Academic Writing

from paragraph to essay

Dorothy E Zemach   Lisa A Rumisek

MACMILLAN

Contents

To the Teacher

Non-native English speakers who enrol in a college or university want to develop writing skills that will lead to academic success. This book is a combination text and workbook. Its focused lessons, specific exercises, and ample opportunities for practice are designed to help your students gain confidence in writing academic prose.

This book is designed to take university-level students with an intermediate ability in English as a Foreign Language from paragraph writing to essay writing. The course combines a process approach to writing (where students work on invention, peer response, editing, and writing multiple drafts) with a pragmatic approach to teaching the basics of writing (with direct instruction on such elements as topic sentences, thesis statements, and outlines).

The Introduction presents process writing to students. The tasks in the main units are graded. Students first work on recognising and identifying key writing structures from model paragraphs and essays. Then they manipulate the structures in short, manageable tasks. Finally, they apply the structures to their own writing. There are opportunities for students to work independently, with a partner, and with a group. The exercises can be done either in class or as homework. Critical thinking is emphasised, so that students become aware of the impact of their choice of words, sentences, and organisational techniques on the effectiveness of their writing. The focus throughout is on academic writing—the type of writing used in university courses and exams in English-speaking institutions of higher education.

In Units 1–6, students analyse and write the types of paragraphs that commonly occur in academic contexts. They practise writing topic sentences and concluding sentences, organising the paragraph coherently, and using appropriate vocabulary, grammar, and transitional devices in the paragraph body. In Unit 7, students write two-paragraph texts, in preparation for longer assignments. In Units 8–11, students apply what they have learned about paragraphs to essay writing. They work on developing and supporting a central thesis, organising an outline from which to write, and writing effective introductions and conclusions. Unit 12 discusses strategies for timed essay writing, including understanding standard instructions, time-management techniques, and methods for organising information.

Included in the Student Book are samples of the development of an essay from brainstorming to the final draft. There is also a guide to punctuation and examples of a letter requesting information, a personal essay of the type commonly required in university applications, CVs and addressed envelopes. Photocopiable exercises and activities are also included.

To the Student

Writing is a very important part of your university study. You will write assignments that may range from one paragraph to several pages long, and will write answers on tests and exams that may be a few sentences long or a complete essay.

Academic writing in English may be different not only from academic writing in your own language, but even from other writing in English. The purpose of this book is to help you recognise and produce the sort of writing that you will do for your university courses.

During this course, you will have many opportunities to study and discuss examples of English academic writing. Naturally, you will also have many opportunities to discuss your own academic writing and the writing of your classmates. You will learn how important the reader is to the writer, and how to express clearly and directly what you mean to communicate. We hope that what you learn in this course will help you throughout your academic studies and beyond.

You should come to your writing class every day with energy and a willingness to work and learn. Your teacher and your classmates have a lot to share with you, and you have a lot to share with them. By coming to class with your questions, taking chances and trying new ways, and expressing your ideas in another language, you will add not only to your own world but to the world of those around you. Good luck!

Introduction: Process Writing

In this unit, you will ...

- **learn about process writing, the writing method used in most English-speaking university classes.**

The writing process

1 These words are important for understanding the writing process. Match each word with the correct definition.

a. step	**1.** to check a piece of writing for errors
b. topic	**2.** a group of related sentences
c. gather	**3.** one thing in a series of things you do
d. organise	**4.** subject; what the piece of writing is about
e. paragraph	**5.** to change or correct a piece of writing
f. essay	**6.** a short piece of writing, at least three paragraphs long
g. proofread	**7.** to arrange in a clear, logical way
h. edit	**8.** to find and collect together

The six steps of the writing process

2 Read about the writing process. These are the steps you will practise in this book.

➲ **Process writing**
When we write, we do more than just put words together to make sentences. Good writers go through several steps to produce a piece of writing.

Pre-writing

STEP ONE: Choose a topic. Before you write, your teacher gives you a specific assignment or some ideas of what to write about. If not, choose your topic yourself.

STEP TWO: Gather ideas. When you have a topic, think about what you will write about that topic.

STEP THREE: Organise. Decide which of the ideas you want to use and where you want to use them. Choose which idea to talk about first, which to talk about next, and which to talk about last.

Drafting

STEP FOUR: Write. Write your paragraph or essay from start to finish. Use your notes about your ideas and organisation.

Reviewing and revising

STEP FIVE: Review structure and content. Check what you have written. Read your writing silently to yourself or aloud, perhaps to a friend. Look for places where you can add more information, and check to see if you have any unnecessary information. Ask a classmate to exchange texts with you. Your classmate reads your text, and you read his or hers. Getting a reader's opinion is a good way to know if your writing is clear and effective. Learning to give opinions about other people's writing helps you to improve your own. You may want to go on to step six now and revise the structure and content of your text before you proofread it.

Rewriting

STEP SIX:
Revise structure and content. Use your ideas from step five to rewrite your text, making improvements to the structure and content. You might need to explain something more clearly, or add more details. You may even need to change your organisation so that your text is more logical. Together, steps five and six can be called *editing*.

Proofread. Read your text again. This time, check your spelling and grammar and think about the words you have chosen to use.

Make final corrections. Check that you have corrected the errors you discovered in steps five and six and make any other changes you want to make. Now your text is finished!

Steps five and six can be repeated many times.

Review

3 **Complete this chart, summarising the steps of the writing process.**

Pre-writing

- **STEP ONE:** Choose a ....
- **STEP TWO:** Gather ....
- **STEP THREE:** Decide ....

Drafting

- **STEP FOUR:** Write ....

Reviewing and revising

- **STEP FIVE:** Check ....

Rewriting

- **STEP SIX:**

May need to ...
- explain ....
- add ....
- change ....

Steps .... and .... may be .... many times.

Pre-Writing: Getting Ready to Write

In this unit, you will learn how to ...
- **choose and narrow a topic.**
- **gather ideas.**
- **edit ideas.**

What is pre-writing?
Before you begin writing, you decide what you are going to write about. Then you plan what you are going to write. This process is called *pre-writing.*

Choosing and narrowing a topic

How to choose a topic for a paragraph
A paragraph is a group of five to ten sentences that give information about a topic. Before you write, you must choose a topic for your paragraph.

- Choose a topic that isn't too *narrow* (limited, brief). A narrow topic will not have enough ideas to write about. *The ages of my brothers and sisters* is too narrow. You can't write very much about it.
- Choose a topic that isn't too *broad* (general). A broad topic will have too many ideas for just one paragraph. Most paragraphs are five to ten sentences long. *Schools* is too general. There are thousands of things you could say about it.

  A student could narrow this topic by choosing one aspect of schools to discuss.
  schools → *secondary schools in my country*
  popular school clubs
  university entrance exams

1 Choose three topics from this list. Narrow each of the three down to a paragraph topic. Then compare with a partner.

a. festivals
b. friends
c. my country
d. dancing
e. cars

Brainstorming

What is brainstorming?

Brainstorming is a way of gathering ideas about a topic. Think of a storm: thousands of drops of rain, all coming down together. Now, imagine thousands of ideas 'raining' down onto your paper! When you brainstorm, write down every idea that comes to you. Don't worry now about whether the ideas are good or silly, useful or not. You can decide that later. Right now, you are gathering as many ideas as you can.

You will learn three types of brainstorming in this unit: *making a list*, *freewriting*, and *mapping*.

Making a list

Write single words, phrases, or sentences that are connected to your topic. Look at this list a student made when brainstorming ideas to write about her topic, 'What should I study at university?'

history—learning about the past
maths (too difficult, not interesting?)
What job do I want later?
English for work? Travel?
writing?
science—biology, chemistry
I don't like physics!
journalism
I like reading—literature?
art—drawing, painting, sculpture
photography?
studying / homework
friends / social life

2 **Work with a partner or small group. Choose one of these topics. List as many ideas as you can in five minutes.**

a. teenage fashions
b. things to do at the beach
c. driving a motorbike

3 **Work alone. Choose a topic from exercise 1 on page 5, and list as many ideas as you can in five minutes.**

Freewriting

When you freewrite, you write whatever comes into your head about your topic, without stopping. Most freewriting exercises are short—just five or ten minutes.

Freewriting helps you practise *fluency* (writing quickly and easily). When you freewrite, you do not need to worry about *accuracy* (having correct grammar and spelling). Don't check your dictionary when you freewrite. Don't stop if you make a mistake. Just keep writing!

Here is an example of a student's freewriting:

> *There are ~~too~~ so many subjects to study at university; it is difficult to choose one. I've always had good marks in maths, but I don't like it very much. I don't like ~~physical~~ physics or any science very much. Writing—I've always liked writing. Would journalism be a good course to take? Newspapers have pictures, too, so maybe photography would be good. I'm ~~maybe~~ definitely looking forward to meeting new friends at university. And what about reading? Reading is a part of any course, but literature includes a lot of reading and it probably includes a lot of writing, too.*

Notice how the writer's ideas jump around. When she makes a mistake, she just crosses it out and continues writing. One thought (*writing*) leads to another (*journalism*), and then to another (*photography*). There are some details that are not exactly about her topic (*looking forward to meeting new friends*), but that's OK in freewriting. You want to get as many ideas on paper as you can. You can take out unnecessary words and sentences later.

4 **Choose one of the narrowed down topics you thought of for exercise 1 on page 5. Practise freewriting for five minutes. Remember, do not stop, erase, or go back. Just write as much as you can.**

Mapping

To make a map, use a whole sheet of paper, and write your topic in the middle, with a circle around it. Then put the next idea in a circle above or below your topic, and connect the circles with lines. The lines show that the two ideas are related.

The example below shows a map of 'What should I study at university?' The writer connected *favourite subjects* to the main idea. *Art* and *English* are connected to *favourite subjects* to show that they are related.

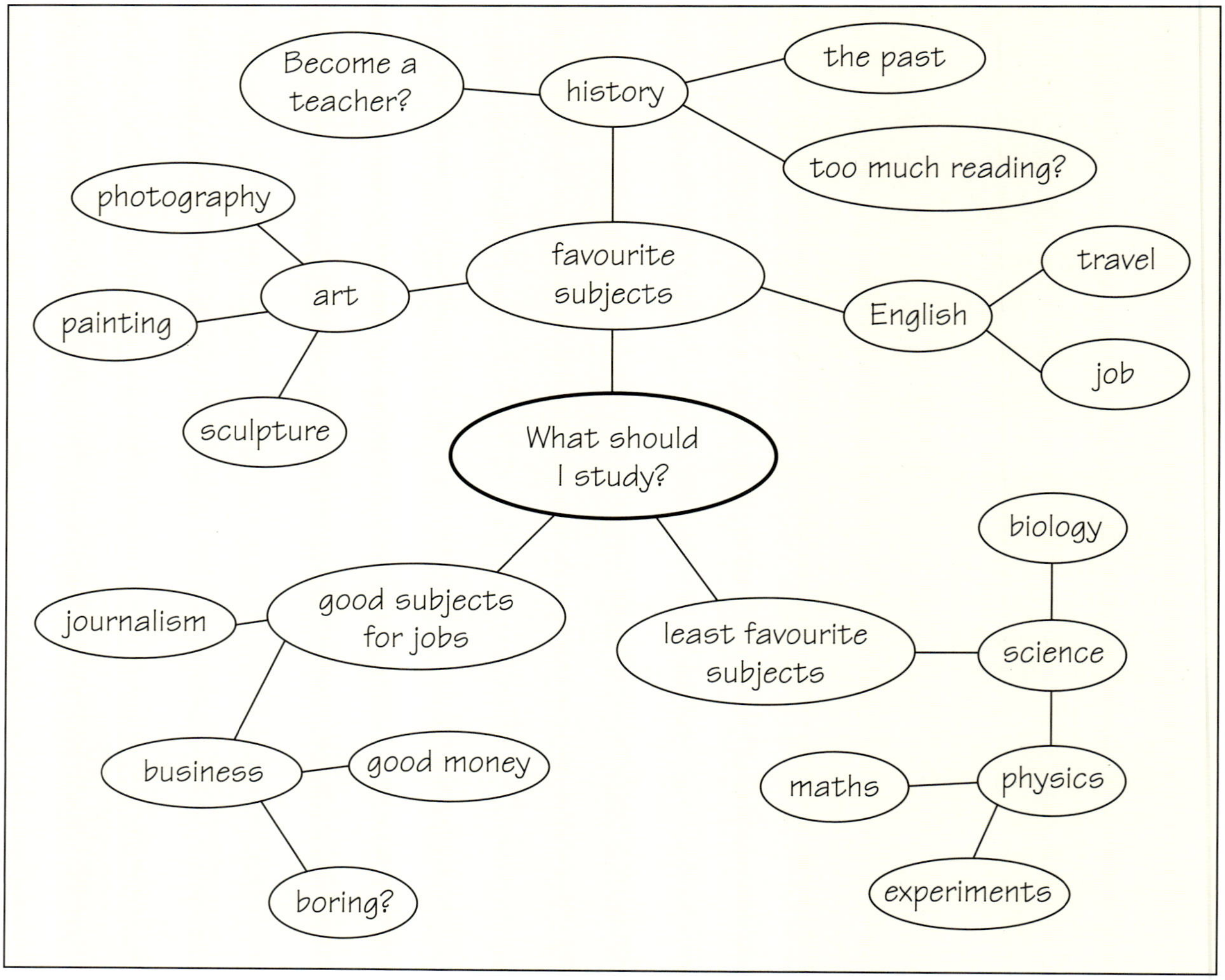

5 **Choose another narrowed down topic you thought of for exercise 1 on page 5. Make a map in five minutes. Share your map with a partner. Explain how the circles are related to each other.**

What's the best way to brainstorm?

There is no best method of brainstorming. Some writers like to use lists because they don't have to write complete sentences. Some writers like freewriting because they can write quickly and ideas come easily. Some writers prefer mapping because they can easily see the relationship between ideas. Experiment with all three methods, and then choose the one that works best for you.

Editing

➲ How to edit

After you have gathered plenty of ideas, you will need to go back and edit them. This is the time to choose which ideas are the most interesting, and which are the most *relevant to* (important or necessary for) your topic. Of course, you can still add new ideas if you think of something else while you are re-reading your list. For example, the student writing 'What should I study in college?' edited her list like this:

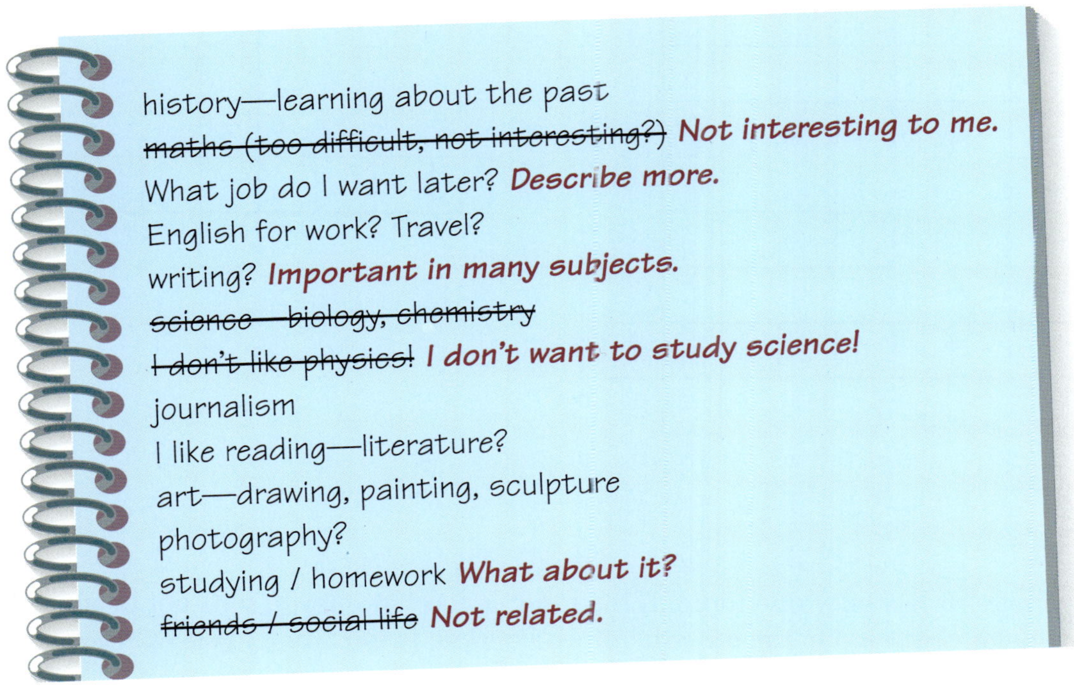

To edit freewriting, cross out sentences or parts of sentences that aren't related. You can add more ideas in the margin or add more sentences at the bottom. To edit a map, cross out circles that don't belong, and add new ones if you get more ideas. You might also change the lines you have drawn.

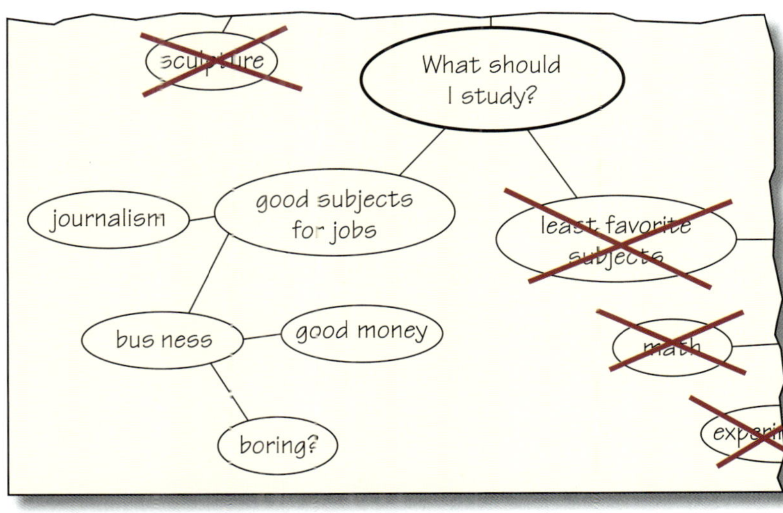

6 **Look at the list you made in exercise 3 on page 6, the freewriting you did in exercise 4 on page 7, or the map you made in exercise 5 on page 8. Edit your brainstorming. Show your work to a partner. Explain how you edited your brainstorming.**

Review

7 **Complete the crossword puzzle.**

Each paragraph has only one topic. If the topic is too [1.] n___, you will not be able to write enough about it. On the other hand, if the topic is too [2.] b___, you will have too many ideas for just one paragraph.

After you choose a topic, you will need to [3.] b___ some ideas to write about in your paragraph. One way to do this is to make a [4.] l___. Another way of brainstorming is [5.] m___. After you have written down many ideas, you can go back and decide which ones are the most interesting and the most [6.] r___ to your topic.

[7.] F___ is a useful way to help you write more easily and naturally. In this kind of writing, you are working on [8.] f___, and not [9.] a___.

8 **Look again at the note about brainstorming at the bottom of page 8. Brainstorm a list of pros (good things) and cons (bad things) about each of the three methods of brainstorming.**

2 The Structure of a Paragraph

In this unit, you will learn ...

- **the definition of a paragraph.**
- **the parts of a paragraph.**
- **how to identify and write topic sentences.**

What is a paragraph?

As you learned in Unit 1, a paragraph is a group of sentences about a single *topic*. Together, the sentences of the paragraph explain the writer's *main idea* (most important idea) about the topic. In academic writing, a paragraph is often between five and ten sentences long, but it can be longer or shorter, depending on the topic. The first sentence of a paragraph is usually indented (moved in) a few spaces.

Understanding a paragraph

1 **Read this paragraph. It is the beginning of an article about Switzerland in a student newspaper. Then answer the questions.**

Switzerland — Something Interesting at Every Turn

By Ken Jones

If you dream of travelling to a country with beautiful mountains, delicious food, wonderful places to go sight-seeing and polite people, you should visit Switzerland. If you look at the map, the first thing you notice is that Switzerland has many mountains, including some of the highest in Europe. Climbing or skiing down the mountains is great fun. Another thing you will notice is that Switzerland shares its borders with five different countries: France, Germany, Italy, Austria and Liechtenstein. In fact, there are four official languages in Switzerland: German, French, Italian and Romansch. All these groups of people make Swiss culture very interesting. Finally, Switzerland has many cities and interesting places to visit. Cities such as Bern have modern buildings like the Paul Klee Zentrum, yet the traditional alpine refuges in the mountains show that the country's old traditions are still alive. All the people, places and things to see definitely make Switzerland a great place for a holiday.

a. What is the topic of the paragraph?

....

b. What is the main idea about the topic?

....

c. What ideas help explain the main idea?

....

....

....

Paragraph organisation

➲ **What makes a paragraph?**
A paragraph has three basic parts:

1. **The topic sentence.** This is the main idea of the paragraph. It is usually the first sentence of the paragraph, and it is the most general sentence of the paragraph.
2. **The supporting sentences.** These are sentences that talk about or explain the topic sentence. They are more detailed ideas that follow the topic sentence.
3. **The concluding sentence.** This may be found as the last sentence of a paragraph. It can finish a paragraph by repeating the main idea or just giving a final comment about the topic.

2 **Read the paragraph about Switzerland in exercise 1 on page 11 again. Circle the topic sentence, put one line under the supporting sentences, and put two lines under the concluding sentence.**

3 **Put a tick (✓) next to the group of sentences that makes a good paragraph. Why are the other groups of sentences not good paragraphs?**

a. ☐

My best friend has many different hobbies, such as skiing, cooking, and playing the piano, and she is very good at all of these activities. For example, she has played the piano for ten years and has won three piano competitions. She also likes to spend time travelling, and she has been to many different countries in the world. She grew up speaking Spanish and English, but now she can also speak French and Italian. I like my best friend very much.

b. ☐

Classes in literature are useful no matter what job you intend to have when you finish university. Books are about life. People who study literature learn the skill of reading carefully and understanding characters, situations, and relationships. This kind of understanding can be useful to teachers and business people alike. Literature classes also require a lot of writing, so they help students develop the skill of clear communication. Of course, a professional writer needs to have this skill, but it is an equally important skill for an engineer. Finally, reading literature helps develop an understanding of many different points of view. Reading a novel by a Russian author, for example, will help a reader learn more about Russian culture. For anyone whose job may bring them into contact with Russian colleagues, this insight can help encourage better cross-cultural understanding. Studying literature is studying life, so it is relevant to almost any job you can think of.

c. ☐

One good way to learn another language is to live in a country where that language is used. When you live in another country, the language is around you all the time, so you can learn to listen to and speak it more easily.

The topic and the main idea

➲ **The topic sentence …**
- usually comes first in a paragraph.
- gives the writer's main idea or opinion about the topic and helps the reader understand what the paragraph is going to talk about.

4 Circle the topic of the sentence. Underline the main idea about the topic.

a. (Switzerland) is a <u>very interesting country to visit</u>.

b. Dogs make excellent pets.

c. A really good place to study is the library at my school.

d. Learning a foreign language creates job opportunities.

e. Football is my favourite sport because it is exciting to watch.

f. One of the most valuable tools for students is the computer.

g. My sister and I have very different personalities.

h. Summer is the best time to travel in my country.

i. My hometown is a friendly place to live.

5 For each of these paragraphs, choose the sentence from the list below that would make the best topic sentence.

a.

....

.... When Ken wanted to enter a good university, he studied hard to pass the examination. The first time he took the exam, he did not do well, and he felt very discouraged. But he knew he wanted to study at that university, so he studied more. The next year, he tried taking the exam again. The second time, he did very well, and now he is studying engineering. I believe Ken is a good role model for me, and he has taught me that never giving up is the best way to succeed.

1. One of my closest friends, named Ken, is a person I can trust.
2. My friend Ken is a very successful student.
3. I admire my friend Ken because he doesn't give up.

b.

.... *Many children begin learning to play football when they are very young. You can often see them playing at school or in the streets around their houses. At secondary school, students may play football in a team and compete in championships. If a player is very good, he might go on to play for a professional team. People in my country love watching football on television and also go to matches whenever they can. Many people have a favourite team or player, and everyone loves to talk about matches and competitions. Football is really like a national sport in my country.*

1. I love playing football, and I hope I can become a professional player one day.
2. There are many popular sports in my country, but the most popular sport is football.
3. Football is a difficult sport to learn to play well.

6 **Write a topic sentence for three of these topics.**

a. a favourite place to relax
b. a grandparent
c. a pet I have known
d. a favourite food to eat
e. playing a musical instrument

topic: ....

....

....

topic: ....

....

....

topic: ....

....

....

Review

7 **These sentences are mixed up parts of one paragraph. Number the parts in order: 1. topic sentence, 2. supporting sentences, and 3. concluding sentence.**

What should I study at university?

a. .... *It wasn't an easy decision, but for the reasons listed above, I have decided to study journalism.*

b. .... *It can be difficult to choose a subject to study at university because there are so many choices, but by considering my skills and interests, I have decided to study journalism.*

c. .... *I have always enjoyed writing, so it is sensible to choose a subject that involves writing. When I begin working, I would like to have the opportunity to travel, and travel is often an important part of a journalist's job. Finally, I am also interested in photography, and pictures are very important in journalism.*

8 **Use words or phrases in the box to complete the sentences.**

concluding sentence	indented	main idea	paragraph
supporting sentences	topic	topic sentence	

a. The .... is usually the first sentence in a .... It gives the .... and the ....

b. The first sentence of a paragraph can be ....

c. The .... come after the topic sentence, and they explain the topic sentence.

d. The .... comes at the end of a paragraph.

3 The Development of a Paragraph

In this unit, you will learn ...

- **methods of paragraph support and development.**
- **how to write concluding sentences.**
- **how to do peer editing.**

Paragraph development

After you have chosen a topic and written a topic sentence, you *develop* your main idea by adding more information to explain what you mean. This unit will explain three common ways to develop a paragraph: giving *details*, giving an *explanation*, and giving an *example*.

Details

1 **Details are specific points that tell more about a general statement. Read this brochure from a health club. Notice the details that help develop the paragraph.**

ATLAS HEALTH CENTRE

You'll love working out at the Atlas Health Centre, and you'll love what it does for you! We have state-of-the-art exercise equipment in large, air-conditioned rooms. You can work out alone or with the help of one of our professional personal trainers. If you like exercising with friends, join an aerobics or swimming class—or even try kickboxing! Our staff nutrition experts are always on hand to talk with you about health issues. When you've finished, you can relax with a whirlpool bath or a sauna. Come and exercise with us at Atlas, and you'll soon be feeling strong and looking good.

2 **In the paragraph above, underline the topic sentence. Below, list the details used to support the topic sentence. Compare your answers with a partner.**

a. ....

b. ....

c. ....

d. ....

e. ....

f. ....

Explanation

3 **An explanation tells the reader what something means or how something works. In this paragraph, underline the topic sentence. Then answer the questions.**

'A stitch in time saves nine.' My mother, who likes sewing, used this simple saying to teach me the value of working on problems when they are still small. Originally, the saying referred to sewing—if you have a small hole in a shirt, you can repair it with one stitch. But if you wait, the hole will get larger, and it will take you nine stitches. This simple sentence reminds me to take care of small problems before they become big problems.

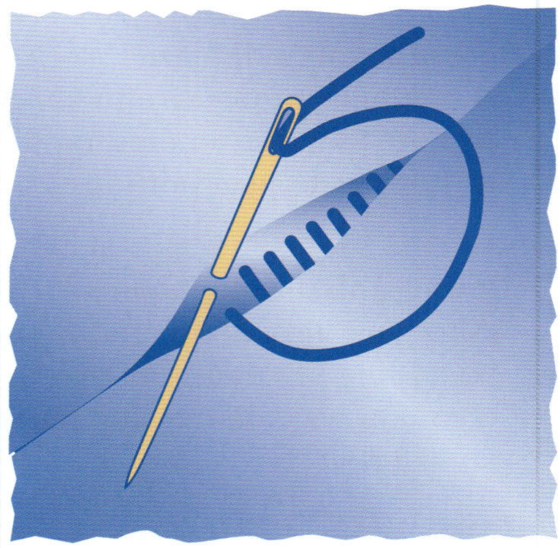

a. What is the writer trying to explain? ....

b. Is she successful? Do you understand the explanation? yes / no

Example

4 **An example is a specific person, place, thing, or event that supports an idea or statement. This paragraph includes an example from the writer's own experience. Underline the topic sentence.**

Even when a first date is a disaster, a couple can still become good friends. For example, my first date with Greg was terrible. I thought he was coming to pick me up at 6.30, but instead he came at 6.00. I didn't have time to do my hair, and my make-up looked messy. When I got into his car, I scraped my leg against the car door and tore my tights. Next, he took me to an Italian restaurant for dinner, and I accidentally dropped some spaghetti on my shirt. Then we went to a film. Greg asked me which film I wanted to see, and I chose a romantic comedy. He fell asleep during the film, and I got angry. Now that Greg and I are good friends, we can look back and laugh at how terrible that first date was!

5 **Why do you think the writer chose to use an example to develop the paragraph in exercise 4 above? Write your reason here, and then compare with a partner.**

....

Choosing a means of support

6 Would you develop each of these topics with details, an explanation, or an example? Explain your choices to a partner. (More than one answer is possible.)

a. what freedom means to me
b. an unusual holiday
c. weddings in my country
d. why I don't like swimming
e. the ideal job

7 Develop your own paragraph. Look back at the topic sentences you wrote in Unit 2, exercise 6 on page 15. Follow these steps.

Step one: Choose one that you would like to develop into a paragraph.
Step two: Brainstorm some ideas using any method you like.
Step three: Develop your paragraph with supporting sentences.
Step four: Exchange paragraphs with a partner. Say what kind of support your partner used. Could your partner tell what kind of support you used?

Concluding sentences

How to end a paragraph
The final sentence of a paragraph is called the *concluding sentence*. It sums up the main points or restates the main idea in a different way. A sentence that sums up the paragraph reminds the reader of what the writer's main idea and supporting points were. A sentence that restates the main idea should give the same information in a slightly different way, perhaps by using different words or by using different word order. A concluding sentence should not introduce a new point.

8 Read the example paragraphs in exercises 3 and 4 on page 18 again. Underline the concluding sentences. Do the concluding sentences sum up the information in the paragraph or restate the main idea?

9 Work with a partner. Take turns reading these paragraphs aloud. Is the main idea developed by details, an explanation, or an example? Is there a concluding sentence? Circle *yes* or *no*. If there is no concluding sentence, write one with your partner.

Even simple study habits can improve your marks. At university I learned how important it is to get enough sleep. When you are well-rested, it is easier to learn. Research shows that when people don't get enough sleep, their memories aren't as effective. If students are really tired, they might even fall asleep in class! It's easy to see how getting enough sleep can improve your performance at university.

a. means of support: ....

concluding sentence? yes / no

....

My favourite subject is psychology. I enjoy learning about the ways people think and behave. I am also interested in learning about the way children's minds develop.

b. means of support: ....

concluding sentence? yes / no

....

I am too nervous to sing karaoke songs with my friends. The last time I tried was on my birthday, when my friends took me to a karaoke club. I told my friends I didn't want to sing, but they encouraged me until I said yes. When I stood up in front of the microphone, I was so scared, I felt dizzy. It was hard to hear the music, and my mouth was too dry to make a sound. I just stood there until a friend jumped up next to me and finished the song.

c. means of support: ....

concluding sentence? yes / no

....

I will never eat dinner at The Little French Bistro again. The restaurant is not very clean. You can see dust in the corners and on the shelves. The food is expensive, but the portions are small. I never feel full after I've finished eating. In addition, the waiters are not very friendly. For these reasons, I will not visit that restaurant again.

d. means of support: ....

concluding sentence? yes / no

....

For me, a friend is someone who accepts you the way you are. A friend doesn't want you to change your personality or your style. I like people who don't care if the people they are with are wearing popular clothes or listening to trendy music.

e. means of support: ....

concluding sentence? yes / no

....

Peer editing

What is peer editing?

Showing your work to another student is a very useful way to improve your writing. This is called *peer editing*. You read your partner's writing and your partner reads yours. You comment on your partner's writing and your partner comments on yours. You might talk together, write comments on a sheet that your instructor gives you, or write directly on your partner's work.

Here is the first draft of the paragraph about the writer's first date with Greg. The writer has shown the paragraph to another student, who wrote some comments.

Topic sentence Even when a first date is a disaster, a couple can still
Developed by example become good friends. For example, my first date with
Can you make this stronger?
Greg wasn't very good. I thought he was coming to pick
When did he come?
me up at 6.30, but he didn't. When I got into his car,
Explain how you tore them. *Tell me more about this.*
I tore my tights. Next, I accidentally got some spaghetti on
What kind of film? *How did you feel about that?*
my shirt. Then we went to a film. He fell asleep during the
Concluding sentence film. Now that Greg and I are good friends, we can look
Good! *The same as the topic sentence*
back and laugh because even when a first date is a
disaster, a couple can still become good friends.

10 Look at the handwritten comments on the paragraph above, and answer these questions with a partner.

- **a.** How many of the comments are statements? How many are questions?
- **b.** Why do you think the peer editor sometimes wrote questions instead of statements? For example, why did she write 'Can you make this stronger?' instead of 'Please make this stronger'?
- **c.** Why do you think the peer editor marked the topic sentence and the concluding sentence?
- **d.** Do you agree with the peer editor's comments?
- **e.** What do you think the writer will do next?
- **f.** Go back to exercise 4 on page 18 and read the paragraph about the date again. Did the writer use the reader's suggestions?

Why do writers use peer editing?

There are two reasons for peer editing. The first is to get a reader's opinion about your writing. A reader can tell you that …

- you should add more details or explanation.
- something is not organised clearly.
- you have some information that is not relevant.
- there is something that is hard to understand.

These comments will help you write your next draft.

The second reason to share writing with others is for you to read more examples of writing. Other people will have had experiences that you haven't. They may show you fresh ways of writing about experiences. Reading their paragraphs and essays can give you good ideas to use yourself in the future.

How do I peer edit?

- Read your partner's work several times. The first time, just read from the beginning to the end. Ask yourself, 'What is it about? What is the writer's purpose?'
- On your second reading, go more slowly and look at specific parts of the writing and make notes.
  - Look for topic sentences and concluding sentences.
  - Note places where you have trouble understanding something, where there seems to be unnecessary information, or where there is not enough information.
  - Let the writer know which parts of the text are especially strong or interesting.
  - Ask questions. This is a good way to let the writer know where he or she could add more information.
  - Circle or underline words, phrases, and sentences that you wish to comment on.
- Don't look for grammar or spelling mistakes. Pay attention just to the content and organisation of the work.

Giving constructive suggestions

11 **For each pair of sentences, check (✓) the one that you feel would be most helpful to the writer. Share your answers with a partner, and explain your choices.**

a. ☐ This is a weak topic sentence.
☐ Can you make this topic sentence stronger?

b. ☐ Did you remember a concluding sentence?
☐ Why didn't you write a concluding sentence?

c. ☐ You didn't write enough.
☐ Please explain more about your holiday. Where did you stay? What did you do during the day?

d. ☐ I'm not sure what this part means.
☐ This must be wrong. I can't understand it.

e. ☐ I think this sentence should come before the next one.
☐ Your organisation is pretty bad. You'd better change it.

f. ☐ Why do you keep saying the same thing over and over again?
☐ I think these two sentences are really saying the same thing.

g. ☐ I can't understand why you're talking about your sister.
☐ Your paragraph is about your brother, but this sentence is about your sister. Are you sure it's relevant?

h. ☐ This is a good paragraph. Nice work! I wish I could write as well as you.
☐ I like your topic sentence because it has a strong main idea. Your example is funny. I wish I could meet your brother!

12 **Read this paragraph aloud with a partner. Then peer edit it together. Then join another pair and share your comments.**

My father is a teacher. I admire him a lot. I am considering becoming a teacher, too. My older brother works for a big company. My father really loves learning, so he is a natural teacher. My father always helped me with my homework. I think I will become a teacher.

13 **Write a second draft of the paragraph in exercise 12 on page 23. Use the comments you and your partner made. Then exchange paragraphs with your partner. Discuss how your versions are different from the original. Do you think the second drafts are better? Why or why not?**

Review

14 **Read these statements. Write T (true) or F (false). If the statement is false, change it to make it true. Then compare your answers with a partner.**

a. .... Details give more specific information than the topic sentence.

b. .... An explanation tells the reader what something is or how it works.

c. .... A detail is usually a short, personal story.

d. .... The concluding sentence uses the same words as the topic sentence.

e. .... The concluding sentence should finish the paragraph with a new idea.

f. .... A peer editor should mark any spelling and grammatical mistakes carefully.

g. .... A peer editor should give some positive comments.

h. .... Peer editing helps the writer, not the reader.

i. .... If a peer editor can't understand something that you wrote, then you know he or she isn't a very good reader.

j. .... A peer editor should be able to identify your topic sentence, main idea, and concluding sentence easily.

4 Descriptive and Process Paragraphs

In this unit, you will learn about ...
- **descriptive paragraphs and reasons for writing them.**
- **organising and writing descriptive paragraphs using adjectives and prepositions.**
- **process paragraphs and reasons for writing them.**
- **using transition words to write a process paragraph.**

Describing people, places, and processes
A descriptive paragraph explains how someone or something looks or feels. A process paragraph explains how something is done.

Descriptive paragraphs

Using adjectives
Adjectives are words that tell us how things look, feel, taste, sound, or smell. Adjectives also describe how you feel about something. Here are a few common adjectives.

shape and size	**atmosphere**	**how you feel**	**appearance**
large / small	cosy	amazed	colourful
wide / narrow	comfortable	surprised	unforgettable
round	warm / cool	happy	beautiful
rectangular	cold / hot	nostalgic	unattractive

A description of a place may answer some of these questions:
- Where is the place?
- How big is it?
- How warm or cold is the place?
- How does the place make you feel? Why?
- What things can you see in this place?
- What colours do you see?

1 **List some words to describe these places.**

2 **Read this description from a travel brochure. Circle the adjectives.**

Niagara Falls, a popular destination for thousands of visitors each year, is a beautiful place. When you stand at the edge and look down at the 188 feet of white waterfalls, you feel amazed at the power of nature. The tree-lined river that leads into the falls is fast-moving, pouring over the edge of the falls and crashing to the bottom in a loud roar. If you want to experience the falls close up, go for a boat ride. You'll come near enough to look up at the roaring streams of water flowing over the edge and feel the cool mist that rises as the water hits the rocks below. Seeing Niagara Falls is an unforgettable experience!

Describing the place around you

Using prepositions

Prepositions tell us how a space is organised. These are some common and useful prepositions:

in front of / behind
on top of / on the bottom of
next to
above / below, underneath

to the right of / to the left of
in the middle of
around
between

3 **Read this paragraph that describes someone's favourite place. Underline the prepositions.**

My favourite place to relax is a small café down the street from where I live. This café is on a small side street and as soon as you see it, you feel like going in. There are three windows on either side of the door, and each window has a small window box with brightly coloured flowers. There is a small wooden door that opens into the café, and as you go in, you can see a dozen small tables all around the room. Even though it isn't a big place, its size makes it very cosy and comfortable. I always like to sit at a small table in the corner near the front windows. From here, I can look at the artwork on the walls and at the pretty green plants hanging from the ceiling. With a strong cup of coffee and a good book, I feel very happy and relaxed in my favourite café.

4 **Write six sentences to describe the place where you are right now. Try to answer some of the questions under 'Using adjectives' on page 25. Use adjectives and prepositions.**

Describing a character

➲ **Describing people**

Here are some common adjectives for describing people:

Personality	*Physical characteristics*
happy, satisfied	big, large, tall
relaxed	small, tiny, short
exciting	thin
nervous	heavy
angry	strong
serious	weak
sad, depressed	brown-, black-, blond-, red-haired
outgoing	light-, dark-skinned
....	....
....	....

A description of a person may answer some of the following questions:

- Who is the person?
- What does the person do?
- What does he or she look like?
- How does the person act—what is his or her personality like?
- How does he or she make others feel?

5 **With a partner, add at least two other adjectives to the two lists above.**

6 **Read this description written by a young woman about her grandmother. Circle the adjectives that describe the grandmother.**

When I was young, I admired my grandmother for her strength and kindness. She was not very big. In fact, she was tiny and very thin. She was strong, though. She lived by herself and still did a lot of the chores around her house. When I was a child, I saw her almost every day, and she and I would talk about everything. She was a very happy person and was always smiling and joking, and she often made me laugh. My grandmother was also very patient, and she would listen to all of my problems. She gave me very good advice whenever I needed it. I didn't need to be afraid to tell her anything, because she never got annoyed with me. She just listened and tried to help. I also liked to spend time with her because she had interesting stories to tell me about her own childhood and life experiences. When I was young, my grandmother was my best friend.

7 **Describe one of these people. Write eight sentences. Try to answer three or more of the questions at the bottom of page 27. Use your imagination!**

8 **Think of a person or place you know well. Then brainstorm your ideas, narrow down your topic, and write a descriptive paragraph.**

Process paragraphs

9 **A process paragraph is a description of how to do something. It explains the steps you need to follow to complete an activity. Read this recipe and do the exercises below.**

Ingredients
two cups of brown rice
one tablespoon of cooking oil
three tablespoons of chilli sauce
three cloves of garlic
one green pepper
one red pepper
one onion
two tomatoes
two spring onions
salt
pepper

Mike's Brown Rice and Vegetables

Brown rice and vegetables is a simple and delicious meal to make. First, cook the rice, following the directions on the packet. Then, cut the vegetables into one-inch pieces. Next, heat the oil, chilli sauce, and garlic in a frying pan. After that, add the vegetables and fry them until they are soft, but still a little bit crunchy. Now it's time to stir in the cooked rice. After stirring the rice and vegetables together, add salt and pepper to your own taste. Finally, put the rice and vegetables into a large bowl and serve it with freshly chopped tomatoes and spring onions on top. Now you are ready to enjoy your delicious brown rice and vegetables!

a. Underline the topic sentence and the concluding sentence of the paragraph.

b. List the steps for making brown rice and vegetables in the order you find them.

1. *Cook the rice.* ....
2. ....
3. ....
4. ....
5. ....
6. ....
7. ....

c. How are the steps in the paragraph connected together? What words do you see that help show the sequence to follow? Underline them.

Transitions

What are transitions?

Transitions are words that connect the steps in a paragraph. Transition words and phrases show the relationships between the ideas in a paragraph. They are not used between every sentence, but are used often enough to make the order clear. Here are some common transition words and phrases that show time order or the order of steps:

first, second, third, etc.	finally	....
next	the last step	....
then	before	....
after, after that	while	....

10 Add other transition words you know to the list above.

11 Choose appropriate transition words to connect the steps in this paragraph about preparing for a trip.

Planning a holiday abroad? Here are some suggestions to make your trip successful. a. ...., find out if you need a visa for the country that you want to visit. Make sure you have enough time to apply for it b. .... you buy your ticket. c. .... you've found out about visas, you should research airfares and timetables. d. ...., look for the best flight for you. Remember, the cheapest flight may stop over in several cities and reduce the amount of time you have to spend at your destination. You might want to fly direct. e. .... you're researching flights, you can also ask your travel agent about getting a good deal on a hotel. It's a good idea to book your flight and hotel early if you're sure of your destination. If you haven't already done it, the f. .... step is to learn about places to visit, the weather, the food, and other details about the country. The Internet can be a very useful source of information. g. ...., on the day of your flight, make sure you go to the airport at least two hours before your flight. Now you are ready to start enjoying your holiday!

Ordering sentences

12 **Order the steps to form a process paragraph. Write 1 next to the first step, 2 for the second step, and so on.**

Introduction to linguistics: language-learning research project

Conduct an experiment to find out whether learners of English use English more correctly in a written test or in informal conversation.

a. .... Next, make a written test that checks the grammar point you are researching. This could be a fill-in-the-blanks test, a correct-the-errors test, or another style. It should have at least ten questions, but it should not be too long.

b. .... After giving the written test, interview each learner individually for about ten minutes. Try to make the interviews informal and friendly. Be sure to ask questions that will encourage learners to use the grammar point you are researching. Record the interviews. (Ask for learners' permission first!)

c. .... After you have counted the errors, calculate the score as a percentage. Do this for the written test and the spoken inteview.

d. .... Next, read the tests and listen to the recordings. Make a note of how many times your chosen grammar point was used, and how many times it was used incorrectly. Do this for both the written test and the recorded conversation.

e. .... Third, find about ten intermediate-level English learners who will agree to take your test. Arrange a time to give the test to each learner.

f. .... Finally, prepare two graphs to compare your results. Did learners make more mistakes on the written test or while they were speaking?

g. ..... First, choose a common English grammar point you would like to use in your research. Ask your teacher for a suggestion if you need help choosing one.

13 **Write a process paragraph about a topic that you know well. First, brainstorm all the steps that need to be followed. Then write the paragraph. Remember to use transitions.**

Review

14 **This paragraph describes a city park, but it doesn't have enough descriptive details. Imagine that you live next to a park. Rewrite the paragraph, adding description, to make it more interesting.**

I live next to a park. The park is large and has trees and grass. There is a lake in the park where you can see people enjoying many activities. There are a lot of places to sit and relax. There are a lot of paths that you can walk on, and everywhere you walk you can see flowers. I really enjoy spending time in this park.

5 Opinion Paragraphs

In this unit, you will learn how to ...

- **distinguish between fact and opinion.**
- **organise and write paragraphs expressing opinions and arguments.**
- **use transition words to express causality.**
- **use modal expressions to make recommendations.**

Facts and opinions
A *fact* is a piece of information that is true: *That film was three hours long.*
An *opinion* is an idea or belief about a particular subject: *That film was boring.*
Writers use facts to support their opinions and to show why they hold their beliefs.

An opinion paragraph

1 Read this letter to the editor of a newspaper. Answer the questions.

Dear Editor,

More people should ride bicycles into town. Last year, seventy-three percent of all workers drove their own car to work. Car traffic in town is terrible, parking places are hard to find, and pollution from cars is a real problem. Citizens who want a cleaner, nicer place to live ought to try this non-polluting form of transport. Cycling is good exercise, too! The city must not allow this problem to get worse. Instead, people should ride bicycles to work and school—and enjoy the health benefits of daily exercise.

Bill Adams
Bellingham

a. What is the main idea of this paragraph? Circle the sentence.
b. What is the writer's purpose? Why did he write this letter?
c. Underline the sentences or parts of sentences that show an opinion.
d. Why do you think the writer included a fact in this paragraph?

2 **Do these types of writing use mostly facts, mostly opinions, or an even mixture of both? Write F for fact, O for opinion, or B for both. Explain your choices to a partner.**

a. .... film review

b. .... advice column

c. .... police report of a crime

d. .... travel brochure

e. .... news report

f. .... book report for a university literature class

g. .... magazine advertisement

h. .... personal e-mail to a friend

3 **Can you think of other types of writing that use opinions? Make a list. Then make a list of types of writing that use facts.**

Use opinions: ....

Use facts: ....

4 **Read these sentences. Write F if the sentence is a fact, and O if the sentence is an opinion.**

a. .... Airfares have become too expensive.

b. .... English is an easier language to learn than Arabic.

c. .... Owls are birds that hunt at night.

d. .... I was born in New York City.

e. .... Exercise is the best way to stay healthy.

f. .... Internet use has increased every year since its beginning.

g. .... Engineering is the best career choice.

h. .... Big cities are dangerous at night.

5 **Write three fact sentences and three opinion sentences.**

a. ....

b. ....

c. ....

d. ....

e. ....

f. ....

6 **Share your sentences with a partner. Decide which of your partner's sentences are fact and which are opinion.**

Modal auxiliaries

Using modal auxiliaries

When you speak, you introduce opinions with phrases like *I think*, *In my opinion*, and *I believe*. In general, these introductory phrases are not needed in writing. They can even make you sound less sure of your ideas. Instead, writers use grammatical methods such as modal auxiliary verbs and transition words to express their opinions. Modal auxiliary verbs show the strength of a writer's opinion or argument.

AFFIRMATIVE:

The city	could	add more cycle paths.	weakest
	should		▼
	ought to		
	has to / must		strongest

NEGATIVE:

The city	doesn't have to	allow more cars.	weakest
	shouldn't		▼
	can't / must not		strongest

7 **Look again at the paragraph in exercise 1 on page 33. Circle the modal auxilaries. How strong do you think the writer's opinions were? Discuss with a partner.**

8 **Read the paragraph below. Circle the most appropriate modal auxiliary in each sentence.**

Dear Editor,

I agree with Bill Adams's opinion in his recent letter saying that people a. *should* / *don't have* to ride their bicycles into town. However, there is one problem with this idea. The roads in town are so narrow and full of cars that you b. *can't* / *ought to* ride safely on them. If people are going to ride bicycles into town, the city c. *could* / *must* make some cycle paths for people to use. Maybe the city d. *could* / *mustn't* charge a small additional tax on fuel to pay for the cycle paths. Motorists have created the problem, so motorists e. *could* / *should* pay for the solution. The city f. *ought to* / *doesn't have to* support cyclists like Bill Adams by making more cycle paths.

Melissa Green
Greatford

Expressing opinions: class survey

9 **Read these statements that express opinions. Add three of your own.**

Name:	....	....	....
1. Smoking must be banned in all restaurants and bars.	☐ agree ☐ disagree	☐ agree ☐ disagree	☐ agree ☐ disagree
2. University students should not have part-time jobs.	☐ agree ☐ disagree	☐ agree ☐ disagree	☐ agree ☐ disagree
3.	☐ agree ☐ disagree	☐ agree ☐ disagree	☐ agree ☐ disagree
4.	☐ agree ☐ disagree	☐ agree ☐ disagree	☐ agree ☐ disagree
5.	☐ agree ☐ disagree	☐ agree ☐ disagree	☐ agree ☐ disagree

10 **Share your statements with three classmates. Say how you feel about your partners' statements by saying, 'I agree' or 'I disagree', and then adding one sentence. Tick (✓) your partners' opinions about your statements.**

11 **Read the opinion paragraphs in exercise 1 on page 33 and exercise 8 on page 35 again. Then write a paragraph about one of the opinions you expressed in exercise 10 above. Brainstorm ideas, narrow down your topic, and then write. Remember to use modal auxiliaries.**

Connectors of cause and effect

How to use connectors of cause and effect for expressing opinions

Because, since, and *so* are connectors of cause and effect. They join two ideas when one idea causes or explains the other. *Because* and *since* introduce the cause or reason, and *so* and *therefore* introduce the effect or result:

cause / reason	effect / result
petrol is becoming scarce and expensive	*we should develop electric cars*

For example:

Because *petrol is becoming scarce and expensive, we should develop electric cars.*
We should develop electric cars, **since** *petrol is becoming scarce and expensive.*
Petrol is becoming scarce and expensive, **so** *we should develop electric cars.*

Therefore is slightly different. It joins the ideas in two sentences:
Petrol is becoming scarce and expensive. **Therefore**, *we should develop electric cars.*

12 **In the examples above, underline the causes. Circle the results. Do the connectors of cause and effect come before the cause or before the result? Share your answers with a partner.**

Punctuation note

- When *because* or *since* begin a sentence, use a comma after the first part of the sentence (the cause).
- When the effect or result comes first, don't use a comma before *because* and *since.*
- A result or effect beginning with *so* is usually the second part of a sentence. Use a comma before *so.*
- Use *Therefore* after a full stop.
- Use a comma after *Therefore.*

13 **Complete this opinion paragraph using *because* or *since*, *so*, or *Therefore*. Add punctuation where necessary.**

Bruce Lee (1940–1973), the greatest action movie star of all time, should be given a lifetime achievement award for his work in films. Bruce died tragically in 1973 a. .... he wouldn't be able to receive the award himself, but his fans all over the world would love to see him honoured. Why was Bruce Lee so great? The fight scenes in his films were amazing b. .... Bruce was always in top physical condition. His body was almost perfect. He was also a great actor. c. .... he started acting when he was just six years old, he was very comfortable and natural in front of the camera. His face was very expressive d. .... he was able to communicate a lot of feeling with a simple look. Bruce always looked good on film e. .... he was so charming. Bruce Lee was a talented actor, a brilliant fighter, and an almost perfect example of physical fitness. f. .... he should receive an award that recognises his great contribution to the art of film making.

14 **Use the connectors of cause and effect in brackets to join these ideas. You may change the order of ideas. You may make one sentence or two. Use appropriate punctuation.**

a. the city doesn't have enough money / we ought to increase council tax (so)

....

b. I'm going to leave my part-time job / I don't have enough time for my homework (because)

....

c. some plants and trees are dying / this summer has been very dry (since)

....

d. many students are graduating with nursing degrees / it might be hard for nurses to find jobs in the future (Therefore)

....

e. my friends all recommend that restaurant / I will try it this weekend (so)

....

15 **Look again at the opinions that were expressed in exercise 9 on page 36. Complete these sentences in your notebook with your own ideas about these opinions. Use appropriate punctuation.**

a. Because ....

b. .... since ....

c. .... so ....

d. Since ....

e. .... because ....

f. .... Therefore ....

Writing an opinion paragraph

16 **Write an opinion paragraph. First, answer this question: *What do I want my reader to think or do?* Then brainstorm ideas and narrow your topic. Use modal auxiliaries and connectors of cause and effect.**

Review

17 **Put these sentences in order to make a paragraph. Write 1 in front of the first sentence, 2 in front of the second sentence, and so on.**

a. .... He was receiving a call.

b. .... My friend and I leaned forward, listening carefully to the film.

c. .... It was very distracting.

d. .... Last night, I went to see a film with my friend. It was a thriller.

e. .... He decided to answer the call.

f. .... We think that people should turn off their mobile phones when they watch a film, or not bring them at all!

g. .... It was very exciting.

h. .... The man next to us had a mobile phone.

i. .... Suddenly, we heard a loud sound—a silly tune.

j. .... He spoke out loud to his friend.

k. .... Mobile phones should not be allowed in cinemas.

l. .... My friend and I felt annoyed.

m. .... At the most exciting moment, the actors didn't speak. Only quiet music was playing.

18 **With a partner, write a paragraph using the sentences in exercise 17 above. Remember to join some of the sentences with connectors of cause and effect and with transitions from the top of page 30. Read your paragraph to another pair. How were your paragraphs the same? How were they different?**

6 Comparison / Contrast Paragraphs

In this unit, you will learn about ...

- **comparison / contrast paragraphs and reasons for writing them.**
- **how to organise comparison / contrast paragraphs.**
- **connecting words used for comparing and contrasting topics.**
- **how to write about the advantages and disadvantages of a topic.**

Paragraphs that compare and contrast

To *compare* means to discuss how two people, places, or things are *similar*: *Both teachers and students need to spend a lot of time preparing for classes.* To *contrast* means to discuss how two people, places, or things are *different*: *One main advantage of a bicycle over a car is that a bicycle doesn't create any pollution.*

Choosing a topic

1 Brainstorm ideas to compare and contrast. Think of people, places, and things. Then compare your lists with a partner.

People: .... and ....

Places: .... and ....

Things: .... and ....

Comparing and contrasting

2 Read Yuko's e-mail message to her friend and answer the questions.

a. What two things does the second paragraph talk about?
b. Is the second paragraph mostly comparing or mostly contrasting? How do you know?

From: yuko@toko.com
To: sharifa@abz.net
Subject: Stratford University

Hello Sharifa

How are you? I hope everything is OK with you. The English course has almost finished now – can you believe it? I was just talking to Yu Peng yesterday and she told me that you're planning to go to Stratford University. That's great. As I'm planning to go to St John's University, we'll be living in the same city!

Have you decided where you're going to live? My parents want me to live with a host family in the city, but I want to live in a shared flat in a hall of residence on the campus. I think they're both good places to live, but a flat in a hall would be better. When you live with a family, you usually have to fit in with their timetable. On the other hand, when you live in a flat in hall you can do what you want when you want. Another difference is that, with a family, you don't have to cook. In a flat in hall, of course, you have to cook for yourself! That would be good for me because I like cooking. My parents have pointed out that all the food is included in the price when you live with a family, but you have to pay extra for this in hall. Plus there could be complications about sharing the kitchen if everyone wants to cook at the same time. However, when you live in a flat in hall, you get to choose what you eat and when you eat it.

I hope I can convince my parents that living in hall would be better for me than living with a host family!

Talk to you soon.

Love

Yuko

Comparative and contrastive structures

Using comparative structures

These words and phrases are used for writing comparisons:

and	*The man* **and** *the woman are tall.*
both	**Both** *of the tables have broken legs.*
both … and	**Both** *my neighbour* **and** *I are selling our cars.*
also	*The shops are closing for the bank holiday. The post office is* **also** *closing.*
too	*Kathy is planning to go to the party, and I am,* **too**.
neither … nor	**Neither** *Joe* **nor** *Steve went to the meeting last night.*
similar to	*Their new computer is* **similar to** *the one my brother bought.*
the same as	*Is the restaurant where you had dinner* **the same as** *the place where I ate last month?*
(just) as + adjective + as	*His coat is* **just as warm as** *the more expensive one.*
likewise	*My parents were born in a small village.* **Likewise**, *my brothers and I also grew up in a small town.*
similarly	*There are many parks to visit in that city.* **Similarly**, *there are several parks in my hometown, too.*

3 Complete these sentences with phrases from above.

a. The architecture of some modern government buildings is .... the type of construction used hundreds of years ago.

b. In recent years, new technology such as mobile telephones has made life more convenient. ...., the Internet has made a wide variety of information available to everyone.

c. .... the rivers .... the lakes are clear and beautiful.

d. The capital city is just .... modern .... the cities in many other countries.

Using contrastive structures

These words and phrases are used for writing contrasts:

more / less + adjective / adverb + than	*Eating out is usually* **more expensive than** *cooking at home.*
adjective + er + than	*My bedroom is* **bigger than** *my sister's room.*
but, while, though	*I enjoy eating fruit for dessert,* **but / while / though** *my friend likes chocolate.*
not the same as	*This book* **isn't the same as** *the one you bought.*
not as ... as	*Some people feel that doing exercise* **isn't as fun as** *watching TV.*
different from	*That style of shirt is* **different from** *the styles most people wear.*
in contrast	*The lakes we swam in were very clean and beautiful.* **In contrast**, *the lakes in my country are polluted.*
however	*The new shop sells its clothing at low prices.* **However**, *other shops have better quality clothing.*
on the other hand	*My boyfriend likes doing sport.* **On the other hand**, *I prefer doing yoga.*

4 Complete these sentences with phrases from above.

a. Some tourists enjoy going on organised tours, ... many other tourists prefer travelling on their own.

b. The two books are very .... each other.

c. The cost of studying in a college or university in Britain is very high. ...., in many other countries, the cost is much lower.

d. Changes in technology are occurring .... quickly .... in the past.

Similarities and differences

5 **Write eight sentences about these two cars. Write about four similarities and four differences.**

Comparison / contrast organisation

➲ **Two methods for organising a comparison / contrast paragraph**

Method 1: Block organisation
First, write about supporting points for the first topic. Then compare or contrast those same points to the second topic. This type of organisation could be outlined like this:

Topic sentence comparing / contrasting two topics (A and B)

Points of comparison / contrast about Topic A

Points of comparison / contrast about Topic B

Concluding sentence

Reading a story in a book is often very different from seeing it as a film. When you read a story, you need to use your imagination. A book usually gives a lot of description about the people, places, and things in the story, so you can create pictures in your mind. In addition, the conversations between people are always written with details that describe how the people look or feel while they are talking. When you read, you use a lot of imagination to help 'see' the characters in the story. However, when you see a film, it is a different experience. When you watch a film, you don't need to use your imagination. The pictures on the screen give all the details about the people, places, and things in the story. The conversations are spoken out loud, so you just listen and watch. The feelings of the people come through their faces, body movements, and voices. Although a book and a film might tell the same story, reading a book and watching a film are very different experiences.

Method 2: Point-by-point organisation

Compare or contrast one point about the two topics, then a second point, then a third point, and so on. This type of organisation could be outlined like this:

Topic sentence comparing or contrasting two topics (A and B)

First point of comparison / contrast (A1, B1)

Second point of comparison / contrast (A2, B2)

Third point of comparison / contrast (A3, B3)

Fourth point of comparison / contrast (A4, B4)

Fifth point of comparison / contrast (A5, B5)

Concluding sentence

Marilyn Monroe and Princess Diana lived at different times in different countries, but their lives had some surprising similarities. First of all, both women had a difficult childhood. Monroe spent many years without parents in an orphanage, and Diana's mother left the family when she was only six. Later in their lives, both women married famous men. Princess Diana married Prince Charles, and Marilyn Monroe married a famous baseball player and later a famous writer. They also had difficult marriages and eventually separated from their husbands. Another similarity between Marilyn Monroe and Princess Diana was that they were both very popular. Diana was called 'The people's princess' because she was so friendly. Although Monroe was famously sexy, she was well-liked because she seemed very innocent. However, although they both seemed to have very happy lives, both women actually had emotional problems and often felt sad and depressed. Monroe went through serious depression and had to go to a hospital for treatment. Likewise, Diana suffered from an eating problem and was depressed during parts of her marriage. A last similarity between Marilyn Monroe and Princess Diana was their deaths at an early age. In fact, they were both thirty-six years old when they died, Monroe in 1962 and Diana in 1997. Maybe their similar life circumstances and lifestyles explain why Princess Diana and Marilyn Monroe also had similar personalities.

6 Read the two paragraphs above then answer the questions.

a. Which paragraph mostly compares and which mostly contrasts?

b. Finish filling in the outlines on page 46 for each paragraph.

Block organisation: Paragraph 1
Topic sentence: Reading a story in a book is often very different from seeing it as a film.

Topic A—reading a book
Supporting points:

1. ....

2. ....

Topic B— ....
Supporting points:

1. ....

2. ....

Point-by-point organisation: Paragraph 2
Topic sentence: Marilyn Monroe and Princess Diana lived at different times in different countries, but their lives had some surprising similarities.

First point of comparison—difficult childhood

A1: ....

B1: Princess Diana—mother left family

Second point of comparison— ....

A2: Princess Diana—married Prince Charles, later separated from him

B2: ....

Third point of comparison— ....

A3: ....

B3: ....

Fourth point of comparison—had emotional problems

A4: Marilyn Monroe— ....

B4: ....

Fifth point of comparison— ....

A5: ....

B5: ....

7 **Look again at the second paragraph in exercise 2 on page 41. Does it use point-by-point or block organisation? How do you know?**

8 **Read this list of details about two popular sports. Then make a list of similarities and a list of differences below. Discuss your answers with a partner.**

Golf	Tennis
played outdoors on a large, open area	a racket is used to hit a ball
played with at least two people	played by pairs of people
clubs are used to hit a ball	played on a court with a net
both men and women play	played outside or inside
very expensive to play in some countries	both men and women play
accuracy is an important skill	fairly cheap to play
few spectators	speed is an important skill

Similarities between the sports

....

....

....

....

....

....

....

....

Differences between the sports

....

....

....

....

....

....

....

....

9 **Write a comparison or contrast paragraph. Use either point-by-point organisation or block organisation.**

Advantages and disadvantages

Writing about advantages and disadvantages

Another way to compare or contrast is to talk about *advantages* (positive points) or *disadvantages* (negative points) of a topic. If you are writing about one topic, it is usually best to discuss advantages and disadvantages in two separate paragraphs. If you are comparing or contrasting two topics, you could organise the paragraph in either point-by-point or block style.

10 Read this paragraph from a school newspaper. List the supporting points. Does the paragraph discuss advantages or disadvantages?

Studying abroad and studying in your own country both have definite benefits for a student. Living in another country can be an exciting experience because everything seems new and different. The challenge of living in a new environment can give you courage and self-confidence, too. If you want to learn another language, living abroad is a great way to do that because you can read magazines or newspapers, watch television programmes, or make friends with people who are native speakers. Another good reason to live abroad is to learn more about another culture. On the other hand, there are also advantages to staying in your own country to study. It is cheaper than living abroad, so you can save more money. Also, in your home country, everything is familiar. You don't need to worry about being taught in a foreign language, and you can understand the culture and the expectations of teachers. Finally, if you stay in your own country, you can be close to your family and friends. So, if you are thinking about where to study, consider all of these benefits and make a decision that is right for you.

11 Write one or two paragraphs comparing or contrasting topics of your choice or one of these.

- action films / romantic films
- the advantages and disadvantages of living abroad
- living in a small town / living in a big city
- doing sport / watching sport on TV
- the advantages and disadvantages of having a job while at university

Review

12 List five words or phrases of comparison and five of contrast. Use them to compare and contrast two things at your university. Share your sentences with the rest of the class.

Comparison	Contrast
....	....
....	....
....	....
....	....
....	....

13 Work with a partner. Separate these ideas into advantages (A) and disadvantages (D).

Studying English

a. .... takes a lot of time

b. .... classes are fun

c. .... grammar is difficult

d. .... useful for talking to people from other countries

e. .... good for using the Internet

f. .... lots of vocabulary to learn

g. .... too many tests to do

h. .... helps to understand English-language films

i. .... my friends like English

j. .... pronunciation is difficult

14 Now, in pairs, one person should write a paragraph about the advantages and the other person should write about the disadvantages of studying English. Add one new idea of your own to your paragraph.

15 Share your paragraphs with another pair of students.

7 Problem / Solution Paragraphs

In this unit, you will ...

- **write about problems and solutions.**
- **use real conditionals.**
- **write a two-paragraph text with linking phrases.**

Problems and solutions
Problem / solution writing first explains a problem and then proposes one or more solutions to that problem. Often this type of writing requires more than one paragraph. In this unit, you will write a two-paragraph discussion of a problem and solution.

Problems and solutions

1 Read the article from a website on page 51. What is the main idea of the first paragraph? What is the topic sentence?

2 Answer these questions.

a. How is the first paragraph developed? What are the supporting ideas?
b. What do the supporting ideas show?
c. What is the main idea of the second paragraph? What is the topic sentence?
d. What solution does the writer offer? What details support or explain the solution?
e. Is there a concluding sentence in the first paragraph? In the second paragraph?

Writing about problems

How to write a *problem paragraph*
A *problem paragraph* describes and discusses a problem issue. The topic sentence names the issue you will discuss. The supporting sentences show why this issue is a problem.

3 Work with a partner or small group. Discuss why these issues are problems. Then add two more issues and discuss them.

a. air pollution

b. traffic

c. overcrowded classrooms

d. ....

e. ....

Deforestation is a serious problem because forests and trees aren't just pretty to look at, they do an important job making the earth's environment suitable for life. They clean the air, store water, preserve soil, and provide homes for animals. They also supply food, fuel, wood products, and paper products for humans. In the past fifty years, more than half of the world's rainforests have been destroyed. Today, the forests of the world are being cut down at a rate of fifty acres every minute! Scientists say that if deforestation continues, the world's climate may change, floods may become more common, and animals will die.

One solution to the problem of deforestation is to use less paper. If you use less paper, fewer trees will be cut for paper making. How can you use less paper? One answer is to reduce your paper use by using both sides of the paper when you photocopy, write a letter, or write an essay. A second answer is to reuse old paper when you can, rather than using a new sheet of paper. The backs of old envelopes are perfect for shopping lists or phone messages, and when you write a rough draft of an essay, write it on the back of something else. A final answer is to recycle used paper products instead of throwing them away. Most schools, offices, and districts have some kind of recycling center. If you follow the three Rs—reduce, reuse, and recycle—you can help save the world's forests.

➲ Using conditional structures

The *first* conditional is a useful way to talk about both problems and solutions:

Fish **will** get *ill* if *factories* **dump** *their waste into streams.*

modal + main verb (will, can, could, should, etc) — **present**

If *you* **eat** *fish from polluted waters, you* **could** *get sick too.*

present — **modal + main verb (will, can, could, should, etc)**

Punctuation note: No comma is needed when the *if*-clause comes second:
People can become ill if they eat the ill fish.

The event in the *if*-clause is possible, or is likely to happen. The event in the result clause would logically follow. There are other types of conditional sentences, but first conditionals are the most common in writing about problems and solutions.

4 **Read the paragraphs on page 51 again. Underline the conditional sentences.**

5 **Complete these sentences by circling the correct form of the verb.**

a. If you *use / don't use* a map when you drive, you *get / could get* lost.
b. Students *do / will do* badly in their exams if they *don't get / won't get* enough sleep.
c. If you *want / could want* to lose weight, *exercise / don't exercise* three times a week and *eat / don't eat* junk food.
d. If you *fly / could fly* there, it *will be / can* faster than taking the train.
e. Many arguments *are / can be* avoided if you *think / will think* before you speak.
f. I *will go / won't go* to that film if I *find / will find* someone to go with me.

6 **Complete these sentences with your own ideas. Then compare with a partner.**

a. If it rains this weekend, ...

b. If the library isn't open tomorrow, ...

c. If petrol prices increase even more, ...

d. .... , I'll call you tonight.

e. .... , you can make a lot of money.

f. .... , I won't go on holiday.

7 **For each topic in exercise 3 on page 50, write one or two conditional sentences that explain the problem. Compare your sentences with a partner. Did you have similar or different ideas?**

8 **Choose one topic from exercise 3 on page 50. Brainstorm more ideas if necessary, then write a paragraph about it. Use conditional sentences.**

Linking problems with solutions

How to link a solution paragraph to a problem paragraph

The first paragraph—the problem paragraph—explains the problem. The topic sentence of the second paragraph—the *solution paragraph*—introduces your solution or solutions. The supporting sentences show how your solution(s) will solve the problem. Use these phrases:

In order to solve these problems, …
To meet this need, …
One answer is …
A second / third / final answer is …
In order to overcome these problems, …
One solution is …
One thing we can do is …

9 **Read the solution paragraph on page 51 again. Circle the linking phrases.**

10 **Work with a group. For each of these topic sentences, brainstorm solutions. Introduce each solution with one of the phrases above. Then think of one more problem together, and give it to another group to discuss.**

a. We must reduce exam stress for secondary school students.

b. Teenagers spend so much time using their mobile phones that they are no longer skilled at face-to-face interaction.

c. In the next five to ten years, experts predict that there won't be enough doctors and nurses to meet hospitals' needs.

d. We need to find ways to protect young children from violence on television.

e. ....

Writing solutions

Finding the best solution

After you have brainstormed solutions to your problem, you need to select the best one or ones to write about in your solution paragraph. A strong solution clearly and reasonably solves the problem. A weak solution doesn't really solve the problem or is not practical or not logical.

11 **With a partner, talk about the solutions that this student brainstormed for her topic. Mark each one *strong*, *OK*, or *weak*.**

Topic sentence: I need more money while I am at university.

.... borrow money from my friends

.... sell some of my things

.... ask my parents for money

.... go busking with my guitar

.... get a part-time job

.... drop out of university and get a full-time job

.... buy lottery tickets

.... ride my bike to university instead of using public transport

.... ask my lecturers for money

.... buy fewer CDs and new clothes

12 **Use at least three solutions from the list in exercise 11 above to write a solution paragraph. Use linking phrases and conditional sentences to explain how the solutions will solve the problem. Share your paragraph with your partner.**

13 **For the problem paragraph you wrote in exercise 8 on page 53, brainstorm solutions. Edit your brainstorming, then write a solution paragraph. Use linking phrases and conditional sentences.**

Review

14 **Look at this list of ideas that a student brainstormed about his topic. Work with a partner to divide the ideas into problems and solutions. Try to add one more problem and solution to the list.**

Topic: getting along with a flatmate

noisy flatmate

make cleaning rota

flatmate is messy

argue about how to decorate flat

fighting causes stress

set aside quiet time for studying

each person decorates half of the flat

talk each week about concerns

problems	solutions
a.	**f.** ....
b.	**g.** ....
c.	**h.** ....
d.	**i.** ....
e.	**j.** ....

15 **Work alone. Use the ideas above to write a problem paragraph and a solution paragraph. Remember to write a topic sentence for each paragraph, and a concluding sentence for the solution paragraph. Use conditional sentences and linking phrases where you can. Then compare your paragraphs with your partner. What parts were similar? What parts were different?**

8 The Structure of an Essay

In this unit, you will learn …

- **the definition of an essay.**
- **how to format an essay.**
- **how to write a thesis statement.**

What is an essay?

An essay is a group of paragraphs written about a single topic and a central main idea. It must have at least three paragraphs, but a five-paragraph essay is a common length for academic writing.

The structure of an essay

The three main parts of an essay

The introduction
This is the first paragraph of an essay. It explains the topic with general ideas. It also has a *thesis statement*. This is a sentence that gives the main idea. It usually comes at or near the end of the paragraph.

The main body
These are the paragraphs that explain and support the thesis statement and come between the introduction and the conclusion. There must be one or more paragraphs in the main body of an essay.

The conclusion
This is the last paragraph of an essay. It summarises or restates the thesis and the supporting ideas of the essay.

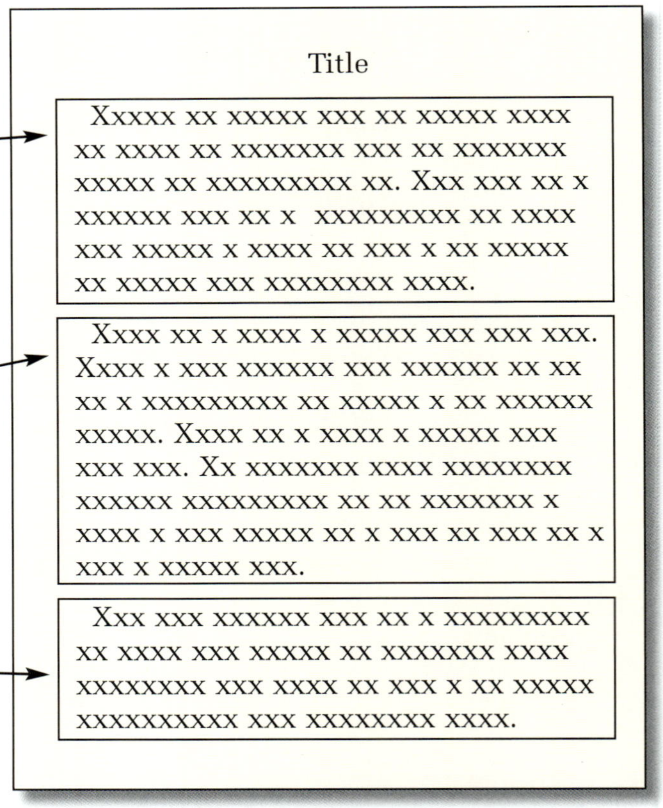

How to format an essay

1. Use double spacing (leave a blank line between each line of writing).
2. Leave 2.5 centimeters (1 inch) of space on the sides, and the top and bottom of the page. This space is called the *margin*.
3. If you type your essay, start the first line of each paragraph with five spaces (one tab). This is called *indenting*. If you write by hand, indent about 2 centimeters ($^3/_4$ inch). Alternatively, paragraphs can begin at the left-hand margin with no indentation. However, you must then leave one line space between each paragraph.
4. Put the title of your essay at the top of the first page in the centre.

I Label the three parts of this essay: introduction, main body paragraphs, and conclusion.

Changing English: the African American Influence

If you ask average Americans where their language comes from, they will probably say 'England'. However, English vocabulary has also been influenced by other countries and groups of people. Some words are borrowed from other languages, such as *typhoon*, which originally came from the Chinese word, 'tai-fung', meaning 'big wind'. *Skunk*, the name of a small, smelly, black-and-white animal, came to English from a Native American language. African Americans, too, have both contributed new words to English and changed the meanings of some existing words.

African Americans, many of whose ancestors were brought to the States as slaves hundreds of years ago, have introduced a number of words to English from languages that they spoke in their native countries. The common English word *OK* is used around the world today, but it was not always part of English vocabulary. One theory is that slaves in America used a phrase in their own language that sounded like *OK* to mean 'all right'. Americans heard the phrase and started using it. Today, almost everyone in the world uses *OK* to mean 'all right'. Another good example of a 'new' word is the word *jazz*. African American musicians living in the United States began playing jazz music in the city of New Orleans, and they used the word *jass* or *jazz* to describe the music and certain kinds of dancing. No one is sure where the word originally came from, but as jazz music became more and more popular, the word *jazz* became a common English word.

The meanings of words sometimes change over time. The word *cool* is a good example. *Cool* has been used in English for a long time to describe a temperature that is 'not warm but not too cold' or to describe a person who is 'calm or unemotional'. However, an additional meaning was given to the word *cool* in the past 100 years. Just like the word *jazz*, African American musicians used the word *cool* to describe the music they were playing. For them, *cool* meant 'good'. As jazz music and other forms of music played by African American musicians became popular, more and more people started to use the word *cool* in conversation. Today, it is still a commonly used word, especially by younger people, to mean 'good' or 'great'. A word with the opposite meaning of *cool* is *square*. Square is, of course, a shape, but it also is used to describe a person who is not cool. This may be because a person who is too old-fashioned and not flexible is like a shape with four straight sides and four corners.

English owes some of its interesting and colourful vocabulary to African Americans. Existing ethnic groups in the United States as well as new immigrants will surely continue to bring new words to English and give fresh meanings to existing words. Who knows what the 'cool' words of tomorrow will be?

Thesis statements

➲ **What is a thesis statement?**
The *thesis statement* is the sentence that tells the main idea of the whole essay. It can be compared to a topic sentence, which gives the main idea of a paragraph. It usually comes at or near the end of the introductory paragraph.

2 **Look at the essay in exercise 1 on page 57 again. Underline the thesis statement.**

3 **In these introductory paragraphs, underline the thesis statement. Then circle the topic and draw another line under the main idea in each thesis statement. Share your answers with a partner.**

a.

Before I travelled to the UK last year, I thought that British food was just fish and chips, roast beef, apple pie, rice pudding and endless cups of tea. These foods are popular in Britain, but during my travels, I discovered that there is so much more to eating in the UK. People from all over the world have made their home in Britain, and they have brought with them their own food. Even in small towns, you can find Chinese, Indian and Italian restaurants, amongst others. The UK can be divided into different regions that each has its own characteristic foods influenced by the culture of the people who live there.

b.

Everybody knows the koala, that sweet Australian animal that resembles a teddy bear. Although koalas look like toys, they are actually strong climbers and spend their days in the treetops. Mother koalas carry their babies around from tree to tree in a pouch, or pocket, on their stomach. Although there were millions of koalas in Australia in the past, they are now a protected species of animal. As a result of human population growth, deforestation and hunting, the number of koalas has declined.

c.

Taoism is an ancient philosophy from Asia that places great importance on the natural world. Taoists believe that spirit can be found in every person or thing, living or non-living. For the Taoist, even a mountain or a stone contains spirit. Lao Tsu, a Taoist writer and philosopher, said, 'People follow earth. Earth follows heaven. Heaven follows the Tao. The Tao follows what is natural'. For thousands of years in China and other Asian countries, gardens have been an important way to create a place where people can feel the spirit of the natural world. Creating a Taoist garden is an art. No two Taoist gardens are exactly alike, but all Taoist gardens include four essential elements: water, mountains, buildings and bridges.

➲ Writing a strong thesis statement

- A thesis statement gives the author's opinion or states an important idea about the topic. It should give an idea that can be discussed and explained with supporting ideas:

  The qualifications for getting into university in my country are unreasonable.

  When studying a foreign language, there are several ways to improve your use of the language.

  These are strong thesis statements. They can be discussed or explained.

- A thesis statement should not be a sentence that only gives a fact about the topic:

  In the Northern Hemisphere, the summer months are warmer than the winter months.

  This is not a strong thesis statement. It cannot be discussed or argued about.

- A thesis statement should not state two sides of an argument equally:

  There are advantages and disadvantages to using nuclear power.

  This could be a topic sentence, but it is not a thesis statement. It gives two sides of an argument without giving a clear opinion of support or disagreement. It could be revised like this:

  Although there are some advantages, using nuclear power has many disadvantages and should not be a part of our country's energy plan.

  This is a strong thesis statement. It clearly gives the writer's opinion about nuclear power.

4 Read these thesis statements below. Write ✓ (strong thesis statement), F (fact only—a weak thesis statement), or N (no clear opinion—a weak thesis statement).

a. .... The top government official in my country is the prime minister.

b. .... Some people prefer digital cameras, while others like traditional cameras.

c. .... India became an independent country in 1947.

d. .... To be a successful student, good study habits are more important than intelligence.

e. .... There are several advantages of owning a car, but there are also many disadvantages.

f. .... Half of the families in my country own a house.

g. .... Using public transport would be one of the best ways to solve the traffic and pollution problems in cities around the world.

h. .... While travelling, staying in a hotel offers more comfort, but sleeping in a tent is less expensive.

i. .... Classical music concerts are very popular in my country.

j. .... In order to create a successful advertisement, it is necessary to consider three issues: who should be targeted, where the advert should be placed, and what type of advert should be made.

Writing thesis statements

How to connect the thesis statement and the essay

The paragraphs in the main body of an essay should always explain the thesis statement. In addition, each paragraph in the main body should discuss *one* part of the thesis. Look at the following thesis statement. The topics to be discussed are underlined:

To create a successful advertisement, it is necessary for advertisers to answer three questions: <u>What are we selling?</u>, <u>Who are we selling it to?</u>, and <u>How can we make people want to buy it?</u>

Possible topic sentences for each paragraph in the main body:

1. *The first step in creating a successful advertisement is to completely understand the product that is being sold and how it can be used.*
2. *A second important part of creating an advertisement is deciding who is expected to buy the product.*
3. *Finally, a way must be found to create an ad that will make people want to buy the product.*

5 **Look at the introductory paragraphs in exercise 3 on page 58. What should the paragraphs in the main body discuss for each thesis statement? Write your ideas and then compare your answers with a partner.**

How to develop a thesis statement

One way to develop a thesis statement for an essay is to write opinions you have about the topic. Begin, *I think that* … and complete the sentence with your opinion. Then remove *I think that* … and the remaining words make a possible thesis statement.

Topic: diet / food
~~*I think that*~~ *a vegetarian diet is one of the best ways to live a healthy life*.
~~*I think that*~~ *governments should restrict the use of chemicals in agriculture and food production*.

After you have written several opinion statements, choose the one that would make the best thesis. Remember to decide if the sentence gives a clear opinion, states a fact, or presents two sides without a clear argument.

6 **For each of these topics, write two or three opinions you have, starting with *I think that*.**

a. exercise

....

....

....

b. university study

....

....

....

c. the Internet

....

....

....

d. music

....

....

....

7 **Now cross out the *I think that* in the statements you wrote in exercise 6 on page 61. Choose the best thesis statement for each topic. Share these with a partner. Decide which ones are good thesis statements.**

8 **Choose one of your thesis statements from exercise 7 above. Circle the topics that must be explained in the essay. Write a topic sentence for each of the circled ideas.**

Review

9 **Complete the crossword.**

The topic sentence gives the [1.] m___ idea of a [2.] p___ . Likewise, the thesis statement gives the main [3.] i___ of an [4.] e___.

The [5.] s___ sentences of a paragraph explain the topic sentence, just as the [6.] m___ ___ paragraphs of an essay explain the thesis statement.

The last sentence of a paragraph is called the [7.] c___ sentence, and the last paragraph of an essay is called the [8.] c___.

9 Outlining an Essay

In this unit, you will learn ...

- **the purpose of an outline.**
- **how to write an outline.**

What is an outline?

An outline is a list of the information you will put in your essay. You can see an example of an outline on page 65.

An outline ...

- begins with the essay's thesis statement.
- shows the organisation of the essay.
- tells what ideas you will discuss and shows which ideas will come first, second, and so on.
- ends with the essay's conclusion.

Writing an outline before you write an essay will ...

- show you what to write before you actually begin writing.
- help make your essay well organised and clearly focused.
- keep you from forgetting any important points.

Imagine your skeleton: although you don't see it, it supports your body. In the same way, although a reader won't see your outline, making an outline in advance will support your essay by providing its structure. In fact, adding more information to an outline is called 'fleshing it out'.

Looking at an outline

1 Read the outline on page 65. Answer the questions.

a. What will the thesis statement of the essay be?
b. How many paragraphs will there be in the main body?
c. How many supporting points will the third paragraph have? What will they be?
d. How many details will the fourth paragraph have? What will they be?

Writing an outline

How to write an outline

Before writing an outline, you must go through the usual process of gathering ideas, editing them, and deciding on a topic for your writing. Writing an outline can be a very useful way of organising your ideas and seeing how they will work together.

To show how the ideas work together, number them. To avoid confusion, use several different types of numbers and letters to show the organisation of the ideas. Use Roman numerals (I, II, III, IV, V, VI, etc.) for your essay's main ideas: your introduction and thesis statement, your main body paragraphs, and your conclusion. Write all of these first, before going into more detail anywhere.

I. Introduction
II. First main idea
III. Second main idea
IV. Third main idea
V. Conclusion

Next, fill in more information for the paragraphs in the main body by using capital Roman letters (A, B, C, etc.). Use one letter for each supporting idea in your main body paragraph. Complete this information for each paragraph in the main body before going into more detail.

I. Introduction
II. First main idea
- **A.** First supporting point
- **B.** Second supporting point
- ... and so on.

Finally, use Arabic numerals (1, 2, 3, etc.) to give details for your supporting points. Not every supporting point will have details, and some points will have several. It is not important to have the same number of details for every supporting point.

I. Introduction
II. First main idea
- **A.** First supporting point
  - **1.** First detail
  - **2.** Second detail
- **B.** Second supporting point
  - **1.** First detail
  - **2.** Second detail
  - ... and so on.

Don't Support Nuclear Energy!

I. Nuclear power is not a good energy source for the world.

II. Very expensive
   A. Nuclear fuel is expensive
   B. Nuclear power stations are expensive to build and operate
      1. Cost of construction
      2. Cost of training workers
      3. Cost of safety features

III. Nuclear materials are not safe
   A. Nuclear fuels are dangerous
      1. Mining fuels produces radioactive gas
      2. Working with radioactive fuels can harm workers
   B. Nuclear waste products are dangerous
      1. Very radioactive
      2. Difficult to dispose of or store safely

IV. There is a great possibility of accidents
   A. Nuclear power stations can fail
      1. Three Mile Island, USA (1979)
      2. Tarapur, India (1992)
      3. Darlington, Canada (1992)
   B. Workers can make mistakes
      1. Chernobyl, USSR (1986)
      2. Kola, Russia (1991)
      3. Tokaimura, Japan (1999)
   C. Natural disasters can occur
      1. Earthquake: Kozloduy, Bulgaria (1977)
      2. Tornado: Moruroa, the Pacific (1981)

V. Because of the cost and the danger, the world should develop different types of energy to replace nuclear power.

2 **Fill in this outline for the essay in Unit 8, exercise 1 on page 57. Then compare with a partner.**

The Changing Vocabulary of English

I. Thesis statement: ....

II. Words introduced by ....

A. ....

1. From an African language

2. Now used all over the world to mean ....

B. Jazz

1. Came from ....

2. Exact origin unknown

III. ....

A. Cool

1. ....

2. New meanings

B. ....

1. Original meaning

2. ....

IV. ....: Existing ethnic groups in the United States as well as new immigrants will certainly continue to bring new words to English and give fresh meanings to existing words.

3 **Label each statement T for thesis statement, M for main idea, S for supporting point, or C for conclusion.**

Title: The Benefits of Yoga

a. .... Develops clear thinking

b. .... Physical benefits

c. .... Improves concentration

d. .... Reduces fear, anger, and worry

e. .... Mental benefits

f. .... Improves blood circulation

g. .... Improves digestion

h. .... Helps you feel calm and peaceful

i. .... Develops self-confidence

j. .... Doing yoga regularly can be good for your mind, your body, and your emotions.

k. .... Makes you strong and flexible

l. .... Therefore, to build mental, physical, and emotional health, consider doing yoga.

m. .... Emotional benefits

4 **Arrange the ideas in exercise 3 above into an outline. Compare your finished outline with a partner.**

I. ....

II. ....

A. ....

B. ....

III. ....

A. ....

B. ....

C. ....

IV. ....

A. ....

B. ....

C. ....

V. ....

Evaluating an outline

The outline checklist

Before you start writing your essay, check your outline for organisation, support, and topic development. If possible, ask a friend or your teacher to check your outline too.

Organisation

- ❑ paragraphs in the right order
- ❑ supporting points and details in the right order

Support

- ❑ each main idea related to the thesis statement
- ❑ each supporting point related to the paragraph's main idea
- ❑ each detail related to the paragraph's supporting points

Topic development

- ❑ enough (and not too many) main ideas to develop the thesis statement
- ❑ enough (and not too many) supporting points for each main point
- ❑ enough (and not too many) details for each supporting point

5 With a partner, check the outline on page 69 for organisation, support, and topic development. What should the author add, subtract, or change in this outline? Share your ideas with another pair. Did you make the same recommendations?

In 1848, gold was discovered in California. People from all over the world rushed to California to look for gold—they wanted to become rich. This was called 'the gold rush'.

The Effects of the California Gold Rush on the City of San Francisco

I. The California gold rush changed San Francisco in ways that we can still see today.

II. History of the gold rush
   A. 1848
      1. Gold was discovered near San Francisco
      2. The US president tells the country there's gold in California
   B. 1864: the gold rush ends
   C. 1849: the gold rush begins as people from all over the world go to California to look for gold. Gold is very easy to find.
   D. 1850s: gold becomes more difficult to find; big, expensive machines are now needed to find gold
   E. Gold rushes in other countries
      1. Australia (1851–53)
      2. South Africa (1884)
      3. Canada (1897–98)

III. Effects on San Francisco today
   A. People still come to San Francisco hoping to get rich
      1. Computer industry
   B. Sightseeing is very popular in San Francisco
   C. San Francisco is still an expensive city
      1. Houses and land
      2. Food and clothing
      3. Many new fast-food restaurants sell cheap hamburgers
   D. Still problems in the city
   E. Technological development is still important
   F. There is no gold mining today
   G. Character of San Francisco today

IV. Changes in California in the 1800s
   A. Population increased—more than 40,000 people moved to California in 1848–50
   B. Everything became more expensive
      1. Houses and land
   C. Problems with crime and violence
   D. Technology to find gold improved

V. The special personality of San Francisco can be traced in part to the famous gold rush of the 1800s.

6 Look at the thesis statement and topic sentences you wrote in Unit 8, exercise 8 on page 62. Write an outline for your essay. Then write the essay.

7 Exchange the essay you wrote for exercise 6 above with a partner. As you read your partner's essay, write an outline of the main ideas, supporting points, and details. Your partner will outline your essay. Discuss the outlines.

Review

8 Write a simple outline of yourself or your life. First, outline only the main body paragraphs. Your main ideas could include physical characteristics, your personality, your habits, your family, places you have lived, jobs you have had, things you like and dislike, and so on.

9 Explain your outline to a partner. Your partner will then add a thesis statement and concluding statement.

10 Join another pair and present your complete outlines.

10 *Introductions and Conclusions*

In this unit, you will learn about …
- **the purpose of an introduction.**
- **types of information in introductions.**
- **the purpose of a conclusion.**
- **techniques for writing conclusions.**

The importance of introductions and conclusions
Unit 8 explained that the introduction and the conclusion are two of the three main parts of an essay. Without an introduction and a conclusion, an essay is just a group of paragraphs. The introduction and the conclusion work together to make the topic and main ideas of the essay clear to the reader.

The introduction

What is an introduction?
The first paragraph of an essay, as you learned in Unit 8, is called the introduction. The introduction …

- is usually five to ten sentences.
- catches the reader's interest.
- gives the general topic of the essay.
- gives background information about the topic.
- states the main point (the thesis statement) of the essay.

The introduction is often organised by giving the most general ideas first and then leading to the most specific idea, which is the thesis statement, like this:

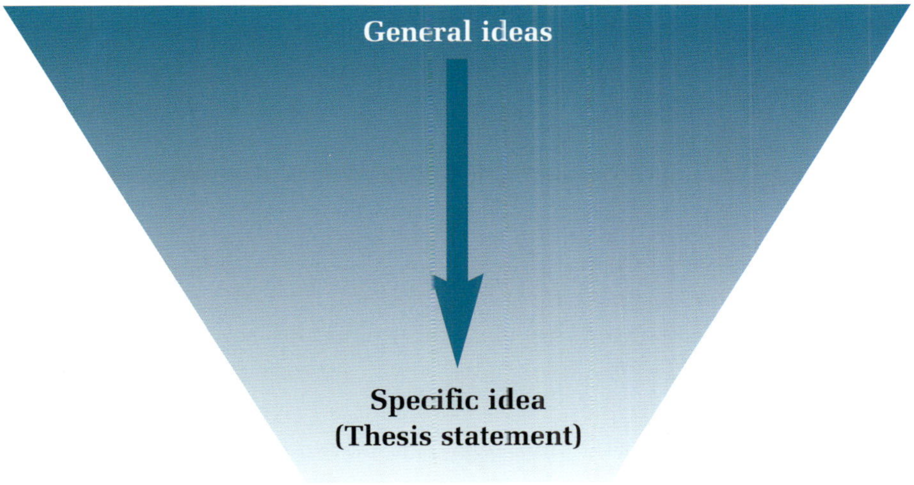

1 **Read the introduction to the essay in Unit 8, exercise 1 on page 57. Complete this diagram.**

General ideas:

Most Americans would probably say that their language comes from England.

....

....

Specific idea (Thesis statement):

....

....

How to write a strong introduction

A strong introduction …

- introduces the topic clearly.
- gives several sentences of information about the topic.
- states the thesis (the main idea) of the essay.

Any of the following will make an introduction weak:

- It doesn't give enough information about the topic or gives too much information about it.
- It talks about too many different topics.
- It does not state a clear thesis.

2 **Read and discuss the following introductions with a partner. Mark the strong introductions with a tick (✓). Mark the weak introductions with a cross (✗). What could the writers do to make the weak introductions strong?**

a. ☐

Family structure has changed a lot in the last fifty years in Asia. The decrease in the number of extended families and nuclear families has caused several social changes.

b. ☐

The number of businesses using the Internet for selling products has increased greatly in recent years. Shoppers, too, are using the Internet in greater numbers to buy all types of products, such as books, cameras, and clothing. Although e-business has become popular, there are certain risks involved in Internet shopping that are a concern for both businesses and consumers.

c. ☐

Stargazing—looking at the stars—is something everyone should try. I love it. When looking at the night sky, most people observe that the moon, planets, and stars move from the east side of the sky to the west over a period of several hours. In fact, this movement is actually the movement of the Earth rotating on its axis. In addition, as the Earth revolves around the sun throughout the year, different stars are visible at different times.

d. ☐

The origins of Irish music can be traced back nearly 2,000 years to the time when the Celts arrived in Ireland. Music thrived under the rule of the Chieftans, but later declined during the British colonisation of Ireland. However, during the Great Famine of the 1840s, thousands of Irish people emigrated to North America in search of a better life, taking their music with them. Irish music soon became established in American cities with a high proportion of Irish immigrants, such as Chicago and Boston. These cities are popular tourist destinations with many interesting sights. However, Irish music really became known to a wider audience in the 1970s, when musicians experimented with more modern arrangements of traditional songs and fusion with rock, world music and jazz. Jazz originated in the American South in the early twentieth century. Now, in the twenty-first century, Irish music is more popular and successful than ever.

e. ☐

Adjusting to another culture's food can be a challenge for many travellers. The geography of a country can greatly affect the typical foods that are eaten by its people.

Types of information

➲ **How to make an introduction interesting**

To make an introductory paragraph interesting for the reader, you can include …

- interesting facts or statistics.
- a personal story or example.
- an interesting quotation.

3 **Read the three introductions in Unit 8, exercise 3 on page 58 again. What types of information does each introductory paragraph contain?**

4 **Look at the introduction of the essay you wrote for Unit 9, exercise 6 on page 70. With a partner, rewrite the introduction, making changes to improve it.**

The conclusion

➲ **The importance of a conclusion**

The conclusion is the final paragraph of the essay. A good concluding paragraph …

- summarises the main points of the essay.
- restates the thesis (using different words).
- makes a final comment about the essay's main idea.
- may emphasise an action that you would like the reader to take.

Don't introduce new ideas in a conclusion. A conclusion only restates or gives further commentary on ideas discussed in the essay.

5 **Look at the essay in Unit 8, exercise 1 on page 57 again. Answer these questions.**

a. Does the conclusion use any of the four techniques described above? Which ones?

....

....

b. Which sentence in the conclusion restates the thesis (from the introduction)?

....

....

6 Match each of these introduction thesis statements with its rewritten version for a conclusion.

a. ...... Supermarkets are the best places to buy food because of their convenience and lower prices.

b. ...... Travelling abroad is a valuable learning experience.

c. ...... Learning to play a musical instrument is very beneficial for children.

d. ...... Creating and owning a business offers more advantages than working as an employee in a company.

e. ...... More houses should be adapted to use solar energy because it is clean and renewable.

f. ...... The World Wide Web can be very useful for research, but it also contains a lot of incorrect information.

1. People can learn many things by travelling to other countries.
2. Despite the challenges, being an entrepreneur can offer more benefits than other types of employment.
3. The fact that larger supermarkets offer cheap prices and a large selection of products makes them the best place for shoppers.
4. The World Wide Web gives access to a huge amount of knowledge, but users shouldn't believe everything they read there.
5. When children are exposed to music and are taught to play instruments such as the piano or violin, there are many positive effects.
6. The sun gives a constant, free supply of clean energy, which more homes should take advantage of.

7 **Read paragraph a in Unit 8, exercise 3 on page 58 again. Choose the best concluding paragraph, below.**

a.

The British eat many different kinds of food, but the typical diet of many people includes eating a lot of fast food and ready-made dishes. The popularity of hamburger and pizza restaurants has increased greatly over the years. As a result of this diet, many British people have food-related health problems. To create a healthier society, people should learn about eating a good diet and should teach their children to do the same.

b.

Clearly, it is difficult to say that there is one type of British food. Every part of the country has its own special dishes based on the produce and tastes of that region. From the Ancient Britons and the Roman, Saxon and Viking invasions to present-day immigrants, the cuisine of the UK continues to change with its changing population.

c.

People who have come from other countries to live in the UK have brought their own traditions and customs with them and added them to British culture. It is possible to find restaurants from all different ethnic backgrounds, especially in larger cities around the country. Immigrants may also maintain their traditions by building places to practise their religion, such as mosques, temples and churches. By continuing to follow some of their customs and beliefs, immigrants can stay in touch with their past while also living a new life in a new country.

8 **Look at the conclusion of the essay you wrote for Unit 9, exercise 6 on page 70. With a partner, rewrite the conclusion, making changes to improve it.**

Review

9 **Complete the crossword puzzle.**

A strong introduction catches the reader's [1] i___. It can do this by including interesting [2] f___, a personal [3] s___, or an interesting [4] q___. It also gives the general [5] t___ of the essay, several sentences of [6] i___ about the topic, and states the [7] t___.

A conclusion [8] s___ the main points of the essay. It also [9] r___ the thesis, makes a final [10] c___ about the essay's main idea, and it may emphasise an [11] a___ for the reader to take.

10 **Write an introduction and conclusion for the outline you created for Unit 9, exercise 8 on page 70. Then exchange these with a partner. Make comments on your partner's paragraphs using the information you learned in this unit about writing good introductions and conclusions.**

11 Unity and Coherence

In this unit, you will learn ...

- **the importance of unity in essay writing.**
- **how to edit an essay for unity.**
- **the importance of coherence in essay writing.**
- **methods of creating coherence.**

Writing effective essays
You've already learned that an essay should be organised into an introduction, a body, and a conclusion. The next step is to make sure that all three parts of the essay work together to explain your topic clearly.

Unity in writing

What is unity?
Unity in writing is the connection of all ideas to a single topic. In an essay, all ideas should relate to the thesis statement, and the supporting ideas in a main body paragraph should relate to the topic sentence.

1 Read the essay on page 79 about Chinese medicine. Then do these tasks.

a. Underline the thesis statement with two lines.
b. Underline each topic sentence with one line.
c. List the supporting ideas in each main body paragraph on a separate piece of paper.
d. After you have finished, review the topic sentences and supporting ideas. With a partner, discuss how the topic sentences relate to the thesis statement and how the supporting sentences relate to the topic sentences. Is the essay unified?

Next Time, Try Chinese Medicine

The last time I had a cold, a friend suggested that instead of taking the usual cold medicines, I visit the traditional Chinese doctor in our city. Although I knew nothing about Chinese medicine, I decided to try it. When I walked in to the Chinese doctor's surgery, I was amazed. It was not at all like my usual doctor's. There were shelves up to the ceiling full of glass containers filled with hundreds of different dried plants and other things I could not identify. Could this really be a doctor's surgery? It seemed very strange to me. When I met the doctor, he explained that Chinese medicine is thousands of years old. The plants in the jars in his office were herbs. These herbs could be mixed together to make medicines. He explained the philosophy of Chinese medicine. The philosophy of traditional Chinese medicine is not the same as the philosophy of modern medicine, but it is useful for curing many health problems.

Modern medicine focuses on illness. If a patient with a cough visits a modern doctor, then the doctor will give the patient a medicine to stop the cough. If the patient also has a fever, the doctor may give a different medicine to stop the fever. For every person with a cough, the doctor will probably recommend the same cough medicine. The philosophy of modern medicine is to stop problems like coughing and fever as quickly as possible. Western doctors usually see illness as an enemy. They use medicines like weapons to fight diseases.

Chinese medicine, in contrast, has a different philosophy. Instead of focusing on a patient's health problems, Chinese medicine tries to make the patient's whole body well again. Specifically, doctors of Chinese medicine believe that inside people, there are two types of energy. The first type of energy, called 'yin', is quiet and passive. The other type of energy, called 'yang', is active. When these two energies are in equal balance, a person is healthy. When there is an imbalance—too much yin, for example—a person becomes unhealthy. A doctor of Chinese medicine doesn't try to stop a person's cough by giving a cough medicine. Instead, the doctor gives a mixture of herbs that will restore balance in the patient's body. As a result, when the body is in balance, the cough will stop naturally.

The Chinese doctor's herbs seemed strange to me at first, but they made me feel better. My cold wasn't cured instantly, but I felt healthy again after a few days. For a very serious health problem, I would probably visit a modern hospital, but the next time I catch a cold, I am going back to the Chinese doctor. Chinese medicine definitely works for some health problems.

Editing an essay for unity

Keeping unity in an essay
One way to keep unity in an essay is to edit the outline for ideas that are not relevant to the thesis statement or topic sentences, as you learned in Unit 9. Likewise, after you have written the essay, it is helpful to review the text and look for ideas that do not relate to the thesis or the topic sentences.

2 **Read this thesis statement and main body paragraphs. The writer has begun to cross out sentences that do not belong. There is still one large piece of the text that should be removed because it isn't relevant to the thesis. Can you find it? Compare your answer with a partner. Then look at the edited version in exercise 6 on page 85.**

Thesis statement: Sign language, the language used by many deaf people, has a 500-year history.

The first sign language for deaf people was developed in Europe in the 1500s. In Spain, a man named Pedro de Ponce was the first person to teach deaf children using sign language. Another Spaniard, Juan Pablo de Bonet, was the first person to write a book on teaching sign language to deaf people. ~~Most of his students were from rich families.~~ Another important teacher who influenced the development of sign language was a Frenchman named Abbé de L'Epée. L'Epée understood that deaf people could communicate without speech. He started to learn the signs used by a group of deaf people in Paris. Using these signs, he developed a more complete French sign language. ~~L'Epée also taught religion classes.~~ Another Frenchman, Louis Braille, also lived during this time. He invented a system of reading and writing for blind people, using raised bumps that can be felt with the fingers. In Germany, a man named Samuel Heinicke was another important teacher of the deaf during this time. However, he did not use sign language for instruction. Instead, he preferred to teach the deaf to understand other people by looking carefully at other people's mouths when they spoke. This is called lip or speech reading.

Speech reading became a popular way of teaching deaf in the United States in the mid-1800s. Alexander Graham Bell, who invented the telephone, was one of the strongest supporters of teaching deaf people to do speech reading. Bell became interested in deafness and teaching deaf people. With his interest in science and the production of sound, he focused on ways of helping the deaf communicate with

more →

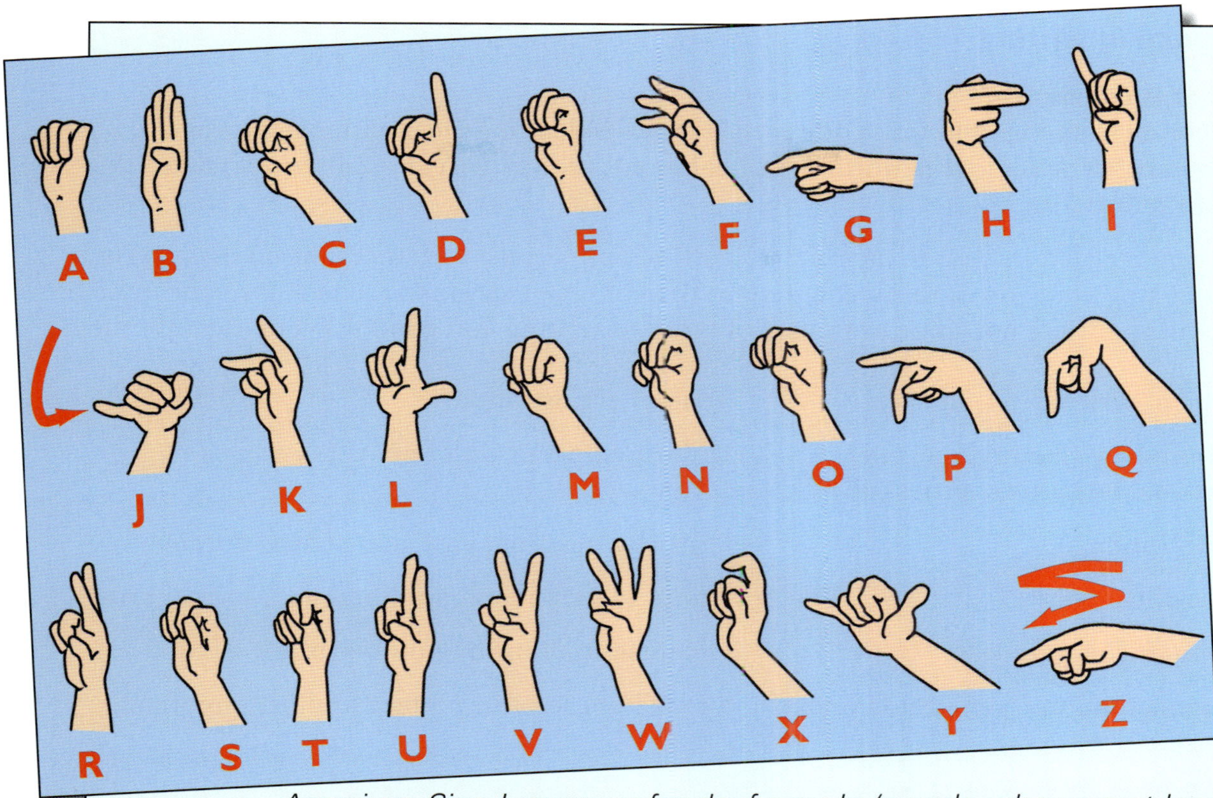

American Sign Language for deaf people (people who cannot hear)

listening tools and speech reading. He eventually opened a training school for teachers of the deaf.

~~Not much is known about the use of sign language among deaf people in the United States before the 1800s.~~ The early 1800s were an important period in the development of American Sign Language. In 1815, a man named Thomas Gallaudet became interested in teaching deaf people. He travelled to Europe to study ways of communicating with deaf people. He was twenty-seven years old at this time, and he studied at a school for deaf students in Paris for several months. In 1817, Gallaudet returned to the United States, and he brought with him Laurent Clerc, a deaf sign language teacher from Paris. Gallaudet started the first school for the deaf, and Clerc became the first sign language teacher in the USA. ~~The school, called the American School for the Deaf, still exists in Hartford, Connecticut.~~ American Sign Language developed from the mixture of signs used by deaf Americans and French Sign Language. Today, it is used by more than 500,000 deaf people in the United States and Canada. ~~About twenty million people in the United States have hearing problems, and about two million of these are deaf.~~

Coherence in writing

➲ **What is coherence?**
Coherence is related to unity. Ideas that are arranged in a clear and logical way are coherent. When a text is unified and coherent, the reader can easily understand the main points.

As you learned in Unit 9, creating an outline helps make a well-organised essay. When organising your ideas, think about what type of organisation is the best for your topic or essay type. Here are some examples of types of writing and good ways to organise them.

Type of writing	Type of organisation
Chronology (historical events, personal narratives, processes)	Order by time or order of events / steps
Description	Order by position, size, and shape of things
Classification	Group ideas and explain them in a logical order
Comparison / contrast	Organise in point-by-point or block style
Argumentation / persuasion and cause / effect	Order from least important to most important

3 **Look again at the essay in exercise 1 on page 79. What type of organisational pattern does the essay use? How do you know? What about the text in exercise 2 on pages 80 and 81?**

Cohesive devices

➲ **What is a cohesive device?**
Cohesive devices are words and phrases that connect sentences and paragraphs together, creating a smooth flow of ideas. In this unit, we'll look at transitions, pronoun references, and repetition of key ideas.

Transitions

As you've learned in previous units, there are many transition words and phrases in English that are used to connect sentences together or relate ideas to one another. Here are several types of writing and some common transitions that are used with them.

Chronology	Comparison	Contrast	Additional information	Examples	Cause and effect	Concluding ideas
before *after* *next* *since* *first, second* *while* *when*	*likewise* *compared to* *similarly* *as … as* *and*	*however* *on the other hand* *but* *yet* *in spite of* *in contrast* *although* *instead*	*and* *also* *in addition* *in fact* *furthermore* *moreover* *Another … is/was*	*for example* *in general* *generally* *for instance* *specifically* *in particular*	*therefore* *so* *thus* *as a result* *since* *because*	*in conclusion* *in summary* *finally* *therefore* *to conclude* *to summarise*

4 Use transitions from the list above, or others that you know, to connect these sentences taken from the essay about Chinese medicine on page 79. When you have finished, compare your answers with the essay.

1. .... of focusing on a patient's health problems, Chinese medicine tries to make the patient's whole body well again. 2. .... , doctors of Chinese medicine believe that inside people, there are two types of energy. The first type of energy, called 'yin', is quiet and passive. The other type of energy, called 'yang', is active. … When there is an imbalance—too much yin, 3. .... —a person becomes unhealthy. A doctor of Chinese medicine doesn't try to stop a person's cough by giving a cough medicine. 4. .... , the doctor gives a mixture of herbs that will restore balance in the patient's body. 5. .... , when the body is in balance, the cough will stop naturally.

Pronoun reference

Two sentences can be connected by the use of a pronoun. A pronoun (*he, she, it, they,* etc.) takes the place of a noun (a person, place, thing, or idea) or a noun phrase (several words that refer to a person, place, thing, or idea). Look at the following example taken from the essay on sign language:

American Sign Language *developed from the mixture of signs used by deaf Americans and French Sign Language. Today,* **it** *is used by more than 500,000 deaf people in the United States and Canada.*

The pronoun *it* refers back to the subject, *American Sign Language,* and connects the two sentences together.

5 **For each of the *italicised* pronouns in this passage, identify the noun or noun phrase to which it refers. Write your answers on the lines below the text.**

Barcelona, Spain's second biggest city and the capital of Catalonia, is a popular tourist attraction for several reasons. First, the city is ideally located for both the mountains and the beach. Although [a] *it* is on the coast, it is only a couple of hours away from the Pyrenees. In addition, Barcelona is both modern and historic. There are many stylish hotels. [b] *It* has a clean and efficient underground system, and visitors can find a variety of shops and restaurants, especially in the Eixample area. The oldest area of the city, the Barrio Gótico, or Barri Gòtic in Catalan, is very beautiful because many of [c] *its* oldest buildings were protected as areas of the city were rebuilt or developed. The most interesting thing about Barcelona may be [d] *its* Catalan heritage. Approximately 70% of the people living in and around Barcelona speak Catalan, a Romance language related to Spanish, and [e] *they* speak Spanish as well. In addition to the strong Catalan background, there are large groups of people who originally came from other parts of Spain such as Andalucía and Murcia living [f] *there*. All of [g] *this* makes Barcelona a great place to visit.

a. it = ...

b. It = ...

c. its = ...

d. its = ...

e. they = ...

f. there = ...

g. this = ...

Repetition of key nouns or ideas

Another way to connect ideas in an essay is by repeating important words and phrases. This will help the reader remember the main ideas in the text.

Modern **medicine** *focuses on illness. If a patient with a* <u>*cough*</u> *visits a modern doctor, then the doctor will give the patient a* **medicine** *to stop the* <u>*cough*</u>*. If the patient also has a fever, the doctor may give a different* **medicine** *to stop the fever. For every person with a* <u>*cough*</u>*, the doctor will probably recommend the same* <u>*cough*</u> **medicine**. *The philosophy of modern* **medicine** *is to stop problems like* <u>*coughing*</u> *and fever as quickly as possible.*

6 **Read these revised paragraphs from the essay on sign language. Underline examples of transition use, pronoun reference, and repetition of key words. Then compare your answers with a partner.**

<u>Thesis statement:</u> Sign language, the language used by many deaf people, has a five-hundred-year history.

The first sign language for deaf people was developed in Europe in the 1500s. Three men in particular contributed a lot to the development of sign language. In Spain, a man named Pedro de Ponce was the first person to teach deaf children using sign language. In addition, another Spaniard, Juan Pablo de Bonet, wrote the first book on teaching sign language to deaf people at about the same time. Another important teacher who influenced the development of sign language was a Frenchman named Abbé de L'Epée. L'Epée understood that deaf people could communicate without speech. He started to learn the signs used by a group of deaf people in Paris. Using these signs, he developed a more complete French sign language.

The early 1800s were an important period in the development of American Sign Language. In 1815, a man named Thomas Gallaudet became interested in teaching deaf people, so he travelled to Europe to study ways of communicating with deaf people. He was twenty-seven years old at this time, and he studied at a school for deaf students in Paris for several months. After that, Gallaudet returned to the United States, and he brought with him Laurent Clerc, a deaf sign language teacher from Paris. As a result of his experience in Europe, Gallaudet started the first school for the deaf, and Clerc became the first sign language teacher in the USA. American Sign Language developed from the mixture of signs used by deaf Americans and French Sign Language. Today, it is used by more than 500,000 deaf people in the United States and Canada.

7 **This paragraph needs more connection. Revise it. Then share your version with other classmates.**

Ho Chi Minh City, in Vietnam, is a fascinating destination for travellers to Southeast Asia. It is located on the Mekong River. It was once an important trading center for the French in Southeast Asia. The influence of French culture can still be felt. Many people, especially the older generations, learned French in school and still can speak it very well. Some cafés serve French-style bread and pastries in Ho Chi Minh City. Expensive hotels and restaurants serve French food. Many of the buildings in the city are built in French style. The Vietnamese and the French fought. The French eventually left the country. There are museums and monuments documenting the country's long—and often bloody—history. If you are looking for a unique city to visit in Southeast Asia, Ho Chi Minh City is an attractive choice.

8 **Write an outline for an essay on one of the following topics or on a topic of your choice.**

a. health and medicine in your country
b. an important problem in your country
c. the importance of technology in society

9 **Edit your outline for unity and coherence, then write the essay.**

10 **Exchange the essay you wrote in exercise 9 above with a partner. Look for the use of the cohesive devices you have learned about in this unit.**

Review

11 **These pairs of sentences need to be joined together to form English proverbs. Choose the best transition word or phrase to connect each pair. Compare your answers with a partner, and then discuss the possible meaning of each proverb.**

a. Don't count your chickens .... they hatch.
1. before **2.** so **3.** because

b. .... life gives you lemons, make lemonade.
1. Before **2.** When **3.** Because

c. Time flies .... you're having fun.
1. after **2.** although **3.** when

d. You can lead a horse to water, ... you can't make it drink.
1. and **2.** but **3.** or

e. Laugh, ... the world laughs with you. Cry, ... you cry alone.
1. and, but **2.** and, and **3.** but, but

f. You don't know what water is worth .... your well is dry.
1. because **2.** after **3.** until

12 **Think of one or two proverbs in your language and translate them into English. Share yours with the class. Then choose one of the proverbs and write a paragraph explaining its meaning.**

12 Essays For Examinations

In this unit, you will learn ...

- **common instructions for essay tests.**
- **techniques for writing timed essays and managing time.**

Essay tests

You may be asked to write essays for tests in your classes, or in entrance examinations for colleges and universities in English-speaking countries. You will have to write essays if you take the TOEFL (Test of English as a Foreign Language), the MELAB (Michigan English Language Assessment Battery), the IELTS (International English Language Testing System) or other Cambridge examinations (University of Cambridge ESOL Examinations). These essays are written at one sitting, in a limited amount of time.

Timed essays

1 You probably already have some experience and ideas that will be useful to you when you write timed essays. Discuss the following questions with a partner or group.

a. Have you ever written timed essays in your own language? Describe the situation(s).

b. Have you ever written timed essays in English? Describe the situation(s).

c. In what situations will you write timed essays in English in the future?

d. What are some ways in which writing a timed essay is different from writing an essay without a time limit? Make a list. Then look at your list and say which aspects might be challenging for you.

e. Do you know any good techniques for writing timed essays? Share them with your partner or group.

Instructions for timed essays

➲ How to write good timed essays

- Check to see how many questions you must answer. Some exams may say *Choose three of the following five topics*. You will not receive a higher score if you write more than three essays—the examiner will probably just mark the first three.

- Check how many points the essay is worth. In a 100-point test, an essay worth twenty points should be longer and more detailed than one worth five points. Spend more time on the longer essays.

- Pay close attention to the instructions for each individual essay question. Be especially careful with questions that have several parts. It is helpful to underline or circle key instructions so that you do not leave anything out.

  Example:
  <u>Which effect</u> of the California gold rush do you think had the <u>biggest impact</u> on the character of San Francisco today? <u>Use examples</u> to illustrate your answer.

- Use some of your time for planning (gathering and organising ideas) and for proofreading your finished essay.

- Always write in complete sentences and pay careful attention to grammar and spelling. Don't experiment with structures or words you are not confident about using correctly.

- Write neatly. Examiners may give lower marks to essays they cannot read easily.

➲ Common instructions in essay tests

compare / contrast
As you learned in Unit 6, compare / contrast paragraphs talk about similarities and differences. You can write one paragraph to compare and another to contrast, or compare and contrast a different idea related to your topic in each paragraph.

discuss
This broad term invites you to describe different ideas about a topic. Organise your discussion around a central thesis statement.

explain, show how
These instructions ask you to show cause and effect. You may also find instructions like these for a problem / solution essay, as discussed in Unit 7.

show, describe, use examples
Make sure that you provide specific details to support your points, as you practised in Unit 3.

which
This word asks you to make a choice. Often a question with *which* will also ask you to defend your choice, for example, *Which solution would you recommend, and why?* Make sure that you clearly indicate your choice in your answer. Don't try to write about each possibility.

2 **Underline the most important part of the instructions in these essay questions. Discuss your answers with a partner or group. Talk about what kinds of information you would include in your answer.**

a. Compare and contrast state and private secondary school education in your country.
b. Think of a story you have read which has also been made into a film. Describe the differences between the two versions.
c. Show how the rise in popularity of communication by mobile phone has changed the ways in which young people communicate.
d. Discuss three results of the Norman conquest of Great Britain in 1066. Which do you feel was the most important?
e. Which environmental problem is the most significant in your community? Explain how your community can solve this problem.

Answering directly

Essay test short cuts
Time is limited, so it is a good idea to take certain 'short cuts' in essay tests. Most importantly, you should write a very short introduction—just one or two sentences is OK—which includes your thesis statement. Do not include the background information you might normally include in an essay. Make sure that your thesis statement directly answers the question. Your answer should show that you know the information that the test asks about. Extra information or any information that is not related to your topic will not help your mark. Your conclusion should also be brief.

3 **Underline the key words of this essay question.**

Which effect of the California gold rush do you think had the biggest impact on the character of San Francisco today?

4 **Tick (✓) the introductions that answer the question in exercise 3 above directly. Write a cross (✗) by the ones that contain unnecessary information or do not directly address the question. Discuss your answers with a partner.**

a. ☐

San Francisco is a fascinating city with a very special character. Each year, thousands of tourists from the United States and other countries visit San Francisco to enjoy its unique style. Many important events contributed to the character of San Francisco, including the California gold rush, the earthquake of 1906, immigration from Mexico, and the rise of the computer industry. But the gold rush was the most important of these events.

b. ☐

The effect of the California gold rush that had the biggest impact on the character of San Francisco today was the damage done by the mining to the rivers and surrounding land.

c. ☐

Experts agree that the California gold rush had an impact on the state of California. In particular, San Francisco was affected by the gold rush. For example, many people came to San Francisco hoping to get rich during the late 1880s. It was a very exciting time.

d. ☐

The California gold rush affected the character of San Francisco in many ways: the population increased, the crime rate rose, land prices went up, rivers were damaged, and people seeking adventure chose San Francisco as their destination.

e. ☐

The character of San Francisco as an adventurous city, a place that attracts risk-takers and thrill-seekers, is the most important effect of the California gold rush of the 1880s.

Managing your time

Write a five-minute outline

Before you write a test essay, write a quick outline. This is the easiest way to be sure that your answer includes all the necessary information and that you don't waste your time with unnecessary information. With practice, you should be able to write a brief outline in no more than five minutes, including the thesis statement and main ideas. Before you write anything else, write your outline at the top of the page. If you run out of time to finish your essay, your instructor will still be able to see your main ideas, and will know that you had a problem with time and not with the content.

Topic: *At university, would you rather live alone, with your family, or with a flatmate? Give reasons to support your answer.*

Sample outline 1:

I. I would rather live with my family to save money.
II. No rent
III. Save money on food
IV. Don't have to pay bills
   A. Electricity
   B. Water
   C. Phone
V. Conclusion: If I save on my living expenses, I will have enough money to pay for tuition and books.

Sample outline 2:

I. *Living alone is the best way for me to learn independence while I am at university.*

II. *Will learn to take care of myself*

   A. *Cook my own food*

   B. *Do my own housework and washing*

III. *Will learn to manage my money*

IV. *Conclusion: University is a time not only to study, but to learn to be an independent adult. Living alone will help me learn how to handle this responsibility.*

5 **Write a five-minute outline for each of these topics. Write a thesis statement, two or more main ideas, and a conclusion. When you have finished, compare your outlines in groups or with the whole class.**

a. Some people like to organise their own trips, and others like to travel on a professionally organised tour. Which do you prefer, and why?

b. Your community is considering building a new shopping centre in the centre of town. Do you support or oppose this plan? Give specific reasons in your answer.

c. Discuss why music is an important part of people's lives.

d. What do you feel will be the most popular career choices for young people in your country in the next five years? Explain your answer with examples.

e. Compare and contrast sending personal letters by e-mail and by post. Which do you prefer, and why?

Write your topic sentences first

Some students like to first write the topic sentence for each main point on the answer sheet, leaving space to go back and fill in the details. If you choose this method, you can add information and examples to each paragraph until you finish or your time runs out. If you run out of time, you may leave out some details, but you won't leave out any main points.

Living alone is the best way for me to learn independence while I am at university.

One of the main benefits of living alone will be that I will learn to look after myself by cooking my own food and doing my own housework and washing.

Another benefit of living alone will be that I will learn to manage my money.

University is a time not only to study, but to learn to be an independent adult. Living alone will help me learn how to handle this responsibility.

6 **For one of the five-minute outlines you wrote for exercise 5 on page 92, write a topic sentence for each main point.**

Checking your work

Check your work

After you finish your essay, or at least five minutes before your time is up, take some time to check your work. Read the essay from beginning to end. Although you cannot read your essay out loud (unless you are alone), try to 'hear' what it would sound like in your head.

- Did you answer all parts of the question?
- Is your essay unified? Cross out any unrelated ideas.
- Are words spelled correctly and written neatly?
- Do your sentences sound clear? If you are not sure if your grammar is correct, try to say your ideas another way.
- Did you erase or cross out any mistakes or stray marks?

7 **You have already spent five minutes writing an outline for the topics in exercise 5 on page 92. Now choose one of those topics and spend another twenty minutes writing the essay. Then take five minutes to check your work. Then share your essay with a partner or small group.**

Review

8 **Work in groups of four. Divide into pairs. Pair A, look at the essay on English vocabulary in Unit 8, exercise 1 on page 57. Pair B, look at the essay on Chinese medicine in Unit 11, exercise 1 on page 79. Do the following:**

a. In pairs, write two or three essay questions about the information presented. Give your essay questions to the other pair.

b. Individually, choose one of the questions the other pair wrote for you and write an answer based on the information given in the essay. You may use your textbook. Write a thirty-minute essay in this way: First, write a five-minute outline. Then, write your essay for twenty minutes. Finally, spend five minutes checking your work.

c. Rejoin your group of four. Take turns reading your essays aloud. After one person reads the essay, the other group members should identify the thesis statement and main ideas. Tell the writer something you liked about the essay.

Additional Materials

Sample essay: brainstorming

Assignment: Write an argument essay of 2–3 pages. First, choose a topic and brainstorm some ideas. Then, organise your ideas into an outline. After you have checked your outline carefully, write the first draft of your essay. Exchange drafts with a classmate, and give and receive peer feedback. Using those comments to guide you, prepare a final draft.

Remember: All final drafts must be typed and double-spaced! Please hand in your brainstorming, outline, and first draft together with your final draft.

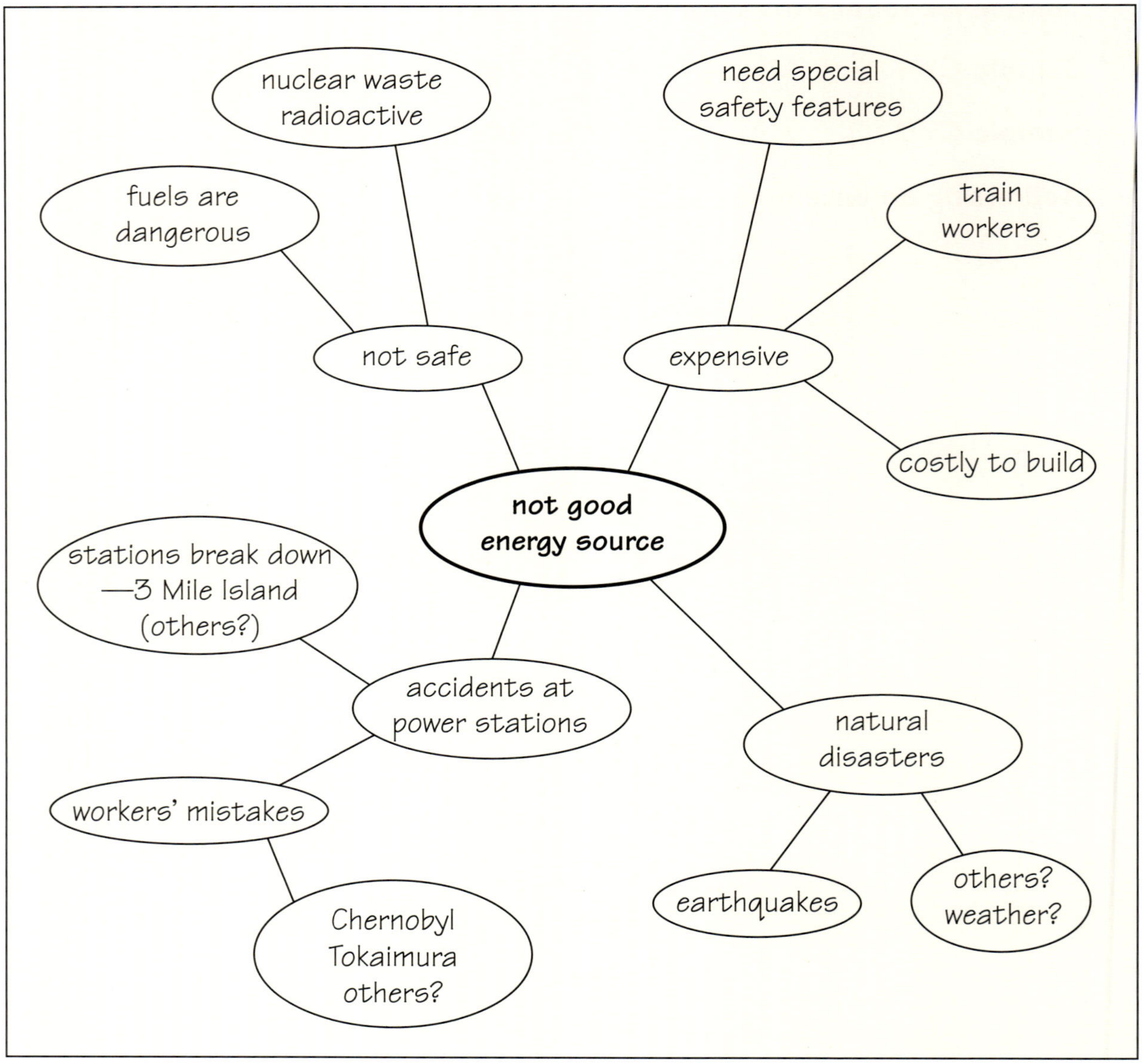

➲ **The outline for this sample essay appears on page 65.**

Sample essay: first draft

➲ **The comments on the essay were written by one of the writer's classmates.**

Don't Support Nuclear Energy!

Can you add some kind of introduction before giving your thesis statement?

Even though it can provide the world with a source of electricity, nuclear power is not a good energy source because it is too expensive, the materials used in the *Good thesis statement—very clear* power stations are not safe, and there is a great possibility of accidents.

Can you add a topic sentence to this paragraph?

First of all, nuclear fuel is expensive. It must be taken out of the ground and transported great distances. As fuels are used up, they will become even more expensive, just as oil and gas have become more expensive. In addition, nuclear *Can you explain this idea a little more?* power stations are expensive to build and to operate. It is expensive to train workers.

Needs transition *You have used 'expensive' 5 times in the paragraph ...*

Nuclear materials are not safe. When uranium is taken out of the ground, radioactive gas is released. This is not safe for the miners. Uranium itself is also not *Why is uranium not safe?* safe. Being around uranium is not safe for workers.

Needs transition

Nuclear waste is also dangerous. It is very radioactive, and it is difficult to dispose of it or even to store it safely. *This is a very short paragraph ...*

Nice transition

<u>Most significantly</u>, there is always a possibility of nuclear accidents. The power stations themselves can fail when they get old or if they are not built correctly. The *Nice specific example* machinery can malfunction, too. In 1979, <u>problems at the Three Mile Island nuclear power station</u> in the United States resulted in radioactive materials escaping into the nearby community. More recently, equipment failures were responsible for accidents *Can you explain what happened at these places?* in power stations in Tarapur, India (1992) and Darlington, Canada (1992).

Can you add a transition?

Workers at nuclear power plants can make mistakes. Perhaps the most famous of these incidents occurred at Chernobyl (in the former USSR) in 1986. Radioactivity from the Chernobyl accident was recorded as far away as Eastern

Good detail

Europe, Scandinavia, and even Japan. Human error was responsible for power station

Are these the only mistakes that have happened?

accidents in Kola, Russia (1991) and Tokaimura, Japan (1999). There is no way we can guarantee that workers will not make mistakes again in the future.

Even natural disasters can affect nuclear power plants. An earthquake in Bulgaria in 1977 damaged the nuclear power plant in Kozloduy, and a big storm in

Can you give some comment about this?

the Pacific Ocean in 1981 washed nuclear waste out into the ocean.

It is true that oil and gas cannot supply all of the world's energy needs much

Good restatement of thesis

longer. However, we cannot replace them with an energy source that is too expensive and is dangerous from the time the fuels are taken out of the ground and even after the station is running.

I think you need some kind of concluding sentence. What do you recommend instead of nuclear power?

Good essay! You have a lot of information and specific examples. Your arguments are very clear. Your organisation is good, too.

Sample essay: second draft

Tian Chan
Academic Writing
Argument Essay, second Draft
15 May 2005

Don't Support Nuclear Energy!

These days, it seems like everyone is worried about how the world will meet its energy demands when we have run out of oil and natural gas. Scientists and researchers are investigating such power sources as solar energy, wind energy, and even energy from hot rocks beneath the earth's surface. However, there is one energy source that I believe should not be developed any further. In fact, I believe that we should stop using it as soon as possible. Even though it can provide the world with a source of electricity, nuclear power is not a good energy source because it is too expensive, the materials used in the power stations are not safe, and there is a great possibility of accidents.

Nuclear power is not an economical energy source. First of all, nuclear fuel is expensive. It must be taken out of the ground and transported great distances. As fuels are used up, they will become even more expensive, just as oil and gas have. In addition, nuclear power stations cost a lot of money to build and to operate because of the great care that must be taken with safety. Because the people who work in nuclear power stations must be highly trained specialists, salaries for workers are also high.

In addition to being expensive, nuclear materials are not safe. When uranium is taken out of the ground, radioactive gas is released. This is not safe for the miners. Uranium itself is not safe either because of its high radioactivity. Because of this, people who work with nuclear fuels are at risk of cancer. As nuclear power stations run, they create nuclear waste, which also is dangerous. It is very radioactive, and it is difficult to dispose of or even to store safely. No town wants nuclear waste buried nearby, and for good reason.

Most significantly, there is always a possibility of nuclear accidents. The power stations themselves can fail when they get old or if they are not built correctly. The machinery can malfunction, too. In 1979, problems at the Three Mile Island nuclear power station in the United States resulted in radioactive materials escaping into the nearby community. More recently, equipment failures were responsible for accidents in power stations in Tarapur, India in 1992, and Darlington, Canada, also in 1992. Both of these accidents led to leaks of radioactive material.

It is not just buildings and equipment which can fail, but people, too. Workers at nuclear power stations can make mistakes. Perhaps the most famous of these incidents occurred at Chernobyl, in the former USSR, in 1986. Radioactivity from the Chernobyl accident was recorded as far away as Eastern Europe, Scandinavia, and even Japan. Human error has been responsible for numerous power plant accidents. Some recent well-known examples include Kola, Russia, where workers accidentally caused an equipment failure in 1991, and Tokaimura, Japan, in 1999. There is no way we can guarantee that workers will not make mistakes again in the future.

Even natural disasters can affect nuclear power plants. An earthquake in Bulgaria in 1977 damaged the nuclear power plant in Kozloduy, and a big storm in the Pacific Ocean in 1981 washed nuclear waste from Moruroa out into the ocean. Of course, it is impossible for people to predict or to prevent events like this. Different types of severe weather or natural disasters can strike almost anywhere in the world.

It is true that oil and gas cannot supply all of the world's energy needs much longer. However, we cannot replace them with an energy source that is expensive and dangerous, from the time the fuels are taken out of the ground to even after the plant is running. Instead, we must develop cheaper and, most importantly, safer types of energy to power our world.

Punctuation

Here are some common rules for using punctuation in your writing. Of course, this is not a complete list. If you have further questions, check a grammar book or ask your teacher.

Capitalisation

Always capitalise:

- the first word of every sentence.
- days of the week (*Tuesday*) and months of the year (*April*).
- the first letter (only) of the names of people and places (*Bangkok, Ayaka Seo*).
- the main words of a title, but not articles (*a, an, the*) or prepositions (words like *to, of, for*) or conjunctions (*and, but*), unless they are the first word in the title:
  The Three Things I Do in the Morning

Full stop (.)

A full stop comes at the end of a statement:

An electronic dictionary is more convenient than a paper one.

Comma (,)

Use a comma to separate a series of three or more items:

I take a dictionary, a notebook and some paper to class every day.

Use a comma before words like *and, but, or, so,* and *yet* to separate two parts of a sentence that each have a subject and a verb.

She needed some work experience, *so* she got a part-time job.
He did not study at all, *but* he still got 87% in the test.

Use a comma after an introductory word or expression, such as *However, Therefore*, and *In conclusion*:

However, the high price of electric cars means that most people cannot afford one.

Quotation marks (‘ ’)

Use quotation marks when you type or write the title of a book or film:

‘Hamlet’ was written by Shakespeare.

When you use a word processor, you can use italics instead:

Hamlet was written by Shakespeare.

Use quotation marks to show the exact words someone said or wrote:

The teacher announced, ‘We’re going to have an exam next week.’
Shakespeare wrote, ‘All the world’s a stage’.

Do not use quotation marks if you’re reporting what another person said:

The teacher said that we should study hard this week.

Note: *That*, as used in the sentence above, usually indicates that the remark is not a direct quotation.

Punctuation when using quotation marks

If you are using expressions like *he said* or *the girl remarked* after the quotation, then use a comma and not a full stop at the end of the quoted sentence:

'We're going to have an exam next week,' announced the teacher.

Use a full stop if the quoted sentence comes at the end:

The professor announced, 'We're going to have an exam next week.'

Notice how a comma is used after *announced*, above, to introduce the quotation.

Full stops and commas are placed inside quotation marks. Exclamation marks and question marks may come inside or outside, depending on whether they are part of the quotation or part of the surrounding sentence:

'Do you know who wrote *Hamlet*?' asked the teacher.
Do you know who said 'All the world's a stage'?

Quotation marks and capitalisation

Capitalise the first letter of the word that begins a quotation. However, if an expression like *she said* interrupts the quotation and divides the sentence, then do not capitalise the first word of the part that finishes the quotation:

'Next week', said the teacher, 'we are going to have an exam.'

The comma after *week* separates the quotation from the rest of the sentence.

Use a capital letter only if the second part is a new, complete sentence:

'We'll have an exam next week,' explained the teacher. 'It will take thirty minutes.'

Advice for academic writing

The following are not usually used in academic writing, although they are fine in informal situations, such as letters to your friends.

- Brackets that give information which is not part of your main sentence:

  Mobile phones are useful (and besides, I think they look great).

  If your idea is important, it should be in a sentence of its own. If it is not important, it should not be in your text.

- The abbreviation *etc* to continue a list. Instead, use a phrase like *such as* in your sentence:

  Students at my university come from countries such as China, India, and Australia.

- Exclamation marks (!). Instead, write strong sentences with plenty of details to show your reader your feelings:

  Angel Falls is one of the most spectacular natural wonders you will ever see.

- An ellipsis (…) at the end of a sentence, to show that the sentence is not finished:

  The teacher said that I should study hard, so …

  Instead, finish your sentence:

  The teacher said that I should study, so I should not go to the party tonight.

Sample information letter

Sender's address → Ulsan-si
352 ponji
Kyongsangnamdo
Yaum-dong
Korea
E-mail hsk@yahoo.com

Date the letter was written → 1 June 2005

Admissions Office ← *Receiver's address*
Central Midlands University
Hunter Road
Wellingham
Shropshire WL2 3YC
UK

Dear Sir or Madam ← *Greeting*

I am writing to express an interest in the pre-sessional English courses at your university, which I learned of while searching the Internet. ← *Introduction*

I would appreciate any information you could provide about your courses. I am interested in studying English for one term, so I would like to know more about the courses you offer, the number of hours of classes per week and the tuition fees.

In addition, it would be helpful if you could provide information about accommodation. I am interested in learning as much as possible about British culture, so if it is possible, I would like to live with a family.

Main body

Thank you in advance for your time and help. I look forward to receiving more information about your courses. ← *Conclusion*

Yours faithfully ← *Close*

Hyun Sil Kim ← *Signature*

Hyun Sil Kim ← *Sender's name*

Sample personal statement

What is a personal statement?
When you apply to a college or university in Britain for an undergraduate or postgraduate degree, you are often asked to write a one-page personal statement. This is a short essay that tells the university why you are applying, and also why you would be a good student to have on their course. The essay below is from a Taiwanese student wishing to do a Master's Degree (MA) in Teaching English as a Foreign Language at Central Midlands University in Britain.

I have been interested in English since I was twelve, when my family took a trip to Australia. I thought then how useful and exciting it would be to talk to the people I met. It was not only the Australians who spoke English, but also other tourists we met who had travelled there from all over the world. Whether they were from Germany, Indonesia, or Brazil, their common language was English, and I wanted to share that language with them.

I worked hard at my English studies at secondary school. I was a member of our school's English Conversation Club, and in my last year I was secretary of the club. I also took part in the national English Speech Contest for three years.

At university, I studied English literature. I also had English conversation lessons at a private school two evenings a week. In addition, I made friends with some of the international students at my university, and we always spoke together in English. During my last two years at university, I took a part-time job tutoring university, primary and secondary school students in English grammar and conversation.

Because of my long interest in English and my experience teaching English, I would like to become an EFL teacher. I have chosen to study in Britain so that I can also learn about the culture of an English-speaking country. I have heard about Central Midlands University from other graduates, and I am impressed with the classes offered there and the quality of the teaching. I think I would be a valuable addition to your EFL course because I could share my own experiences of learning English. I look forward to the opportunity to further my own knowledge of English and of British culture, and to meeting the challenges of both learning and teaching with the other students on the course.

Sample CV 1

Ibtisam Barwani
PO Box 533
Muscat 110
Oman

Tel 00 968 24413 558
E-mail ibarwani@omanmail.com

EDUCATION:

9/97-6/00	Sultan Qaboos University, Oman	BSc in Management and Information
5/97-present	Universal English School	Studying business and conversational English
9/95-6/97	Omani High School, Muscat	A levels in Business Studies, Economics and IT

EXPERIENCE:

6/03-present	Al-Amry Irrigation Company	Assistant IT Manager
10/00-5/03	The British Council, Oman	IT Coordinator

SPECIAL SKILLS:

- Webmaster (3 years' experience)
- Native Arabic, advanced spoken and written English

REFERENCES:

Available upon request.

Sample CV 2

Tao Wang
401 Hui Xin Dong Li Block 4
Chao Yang District
Beijing
China 100029

Tel (00 86) 1064942572
E-mail tw29@sina.com

WORK OBJECTIVE

To obtain a job working in management and marketing for an international company.

EDUCATION

University of Central Wales	June 2004	MSc in Business Administration
Beijing University, China	Feb 2000	BA in Business Studies

OTHER QUALIFICATIONS

Cymru Business Centre, Newtown	Nov 2003	European Computer Driving Licence
English Language Institute, University of Central Wales	Sept 2003	Certificate from the English for University Studies Pre-sessional Course

WORK EXPERIENCE

University of Central Wales	Sept 2003-April 2004	IT Help Desk Assistant

- Responsible for answering queries at the IT Help Desk.
- Provided assistance for students using the university computer rooms.
- Assisted in maintaining equipment.

Lian Wen, Da Lian, China	April 2000-June 2003	Personal Assistant to the Managing Director

- Responsible for sales and delivery of farming materials and supplies to farmers.
- Conducted banking and financial transactions, including payroll distribution.
- Coordinated and supervised staff of 10 in premises and materials management.
- Developed and analysed marketing strategies for the sales of agricultural products.
- Arranged and executed the purchase of inventory essential to business.

ADDITIONAL SKILLS

Languages Chinese (native), English (fluent, both written and oral)
Computer Microsoft Office, Lexis-Nexis, Internet applications

Addressing an envelope

➲ **For a business letter:**

Ms Elizabeth Berriman
Director
English Language Institute
Newington University
Longbridge Campus
London Road
Hants NW2 9LA
UK

➲ **For a friendly letter:**

Karen Armstrong
9 Kennet Road
Reading
Berks RG3 2BN
UK

NB The writer's name and address can be written on the back of the envelope, at the top.
Now, address an envelope from you to the following person:
Mr Peter Saunders, Head of School, School of Business, University of North Wales, Machynlleth, Powys, Wales MC1 2XL

Answer Key

Introduction: Process Writing

The writing process

1

a. 3 b. 4 c. 8 d. 7
e. 2 f. 6 g. 1 h. 5

Review

3

Pre-writing
- Step one: Choose a *topic.*
- Step two: Gather *ideas.*
- Step three: Decide *which ideas you want to use and where to use them.*

Drafting
- Step four: Write *your paragraph or essay.*

Reviewing and revising
- Step five: Check *what you have written.*

Rewriting
- Step six: May need to ...
  - explain *something more clearly*
  - add *more details*
  - Change *your organisation.*

Steps *5* and *6* may be *repeated* many times.

1 Pre-Writing: Getting Ready to Write

Choosing and narrowing down a topic

1

Answers will vary. Possible answers:

a. festivals: The New Year's celebration in my country
The origin of Halloween
b. friends: My best friend at secondary school
How to be a good friend
c. my country: A typical dish from my country
The seasons in my country
d. dancing: Why I love dancing salsa
Studying ballet taught me discipline
e. cars: How I learnt to drive
My favourite kind of car

Brainstorming and editing

2-6 Answers will vary.

Review

7

1. narrow
2. broad
3. brainstorm
4. list
5. mapping
6. relevant
7. freewriting
8. fluency
9. accuracy

2 The Structure of a Paragraph

Understanding a paragraph

1

a. Switzerland
b. It is a country with beautiful mountains, delicious food, wonderful places to go sightseeing and polite people.
c. • Many mountains – climbing them and skiing down them is fun.
• Borders with five countries – France, Germany, Italy, Austria and Liechtenstein.
• Four languages – German, French, Italian and Romansch.
• Many cities and interesting places to visit.

Paragraph organisation

2

If you dream of travelling to a country with beautiful mountains, delicious food, wonderful places to go sightseeing and polite people you should visit Switzerland.
<u>If you look at the map, the first thing you notice is that Switzerland has many mountains, including some of the highest in Europe. Climbing or skiing down the mountains is great fun. Another thing you will notice is that Switzerland shares its borders with five different countries: France, Germany, Italy, Austria and Liechtenstein. In fact, there are four official languages in Switzerland: German, French, Italian and Romansch. All these groups of people make Swiss culture very interesting. Finally, Switzerland has many cities and interesting places to visit. Cities such as Bern have modern buildings like the Paul Klee Zentrum, yet the traditional alpine refuges in the mountains show that the country's old traditions are still alive</u>.

All the people, places and things to see definitely make Switzerland a great place for a holiday.

3

Paragraph *b* is the good paragraph. It has a clear topic sentence, it has several supporting ideas that connect well to the topic sentence, and it has a clear concluding sentence.

Problems with paragraph *a*:

- Not enough supporting sentences to explain the various hobbies mentioned in the topic sentence;
- The sentences about travelling and speaking different languages are not connected to the topic sentence.

Problems with paragraph *c*:

- Not enough supporting ideas to explain the topic sentence;
- No concluding sentence.

The topic and the main idea

4

a. Switzerland is a very interesting country to visit.

b. Dogs make excellent pets.

c. A really good place to study is the library at my school.

d. Learning a foreign language creates job opportunities.

e. Football is my favourite sport because it is exciting to watch.

f. One of the most valuable tools for students is the computer.

g. My sister and I have very different personalities.

h. Summer is the best time to travel in my country.

i. My hometown is a friendly place to live.

5

a. 3 b. 2

6

Answers will vary.

Review

7

a. 3 b. 1 c. 2

8

a. topic sentence; paragraph; topic; main idea
b. indented
c. supporting sentences
d. concluding sentence

3 The Development of a Paragraph

Details

2

The topic sentence is the first one, *You'll love working out at the Atlas Health Centre, and you'll love what it does for you!*

a. state-of-the-art exercise equipment
b. large, air-conditioned rooms
c. work out alone or with trainers
d. staff nutrition experts
e. aerobics, swimming, and kickboxing classes
f. whirlpool bath and sauna

Explanation

3

The topic sentence is the second one, *My mother, who likes sewing, used this simple saying to teach me the value of working on problems when they are still small.*

a. The writer is trying to explain the meaning of the saying 'A stitch in time saves nine'.
b. Answers will vary.

Example

4

The topic sentence is the first one, *Even when a first date is a disaster, a couple can still become friends.*

5

Answers will vary.
Possible answers:
Because the writer had had a personal experience that illustrated the topic sentence; because the writer's personal story was funny and interesting; etc.

Choosing a means of support

6

Answers will vary.
Possible answers:
a. explanation; example
b. details; example
c. details
d. example; details
e. details; explanation

7
Answers will vary.

Concluding sentences

8
Exercise 3, concluding sentence: *This simple sentence reminds me to make small repairs as soon as I can.* It restates the topic sentence.
Exercise 4, concluding sentence: *Now that Greg and I are good friends, we can look back and laugh at how terrible that first date was!* It sums up the information in the paragraph.

9
New concluding sentences will vary. Possible answers are provided below.
a. means of support: example
concluding sentence: yes (restates the topic sentence)
b. means of support: details
concluding sentence: no
new concluding sentence: *Learning about how the mind works makes psychology my favourite subject.* (sums up the information)
c. means of support: example
concluding sentence: no
new concluding sentence: *I will never try to sing karaoke again!* (sums up the information)
d. means of support: details
concluding sentence: yes (both sums up the information and restates the topic sentence)
e. means of support: explanation
concluding sentence: no
new concluding sentence: *Someone who likes me the way I am is a good friend for me.* (restates the topic sentence)

Peer editing

10
a. Seven comments are statements; four are questions.
b. Questions are softer and more polite; questions let the writer decide what to do.
c. To let the writer know that they could be easily identified.
d. Answers will vary.
e. The writer should read the comments, make some changes, and rewrite the paragraph.
f. Yes, the writer did use the suggestions.

Giving constructive suggestions

11
In items a–g, the best choices are the most polite. For item h, the most helpful comment is the one that tells the writer why the paragraph was effective.
a. Can you make this topic sentence stronger?
b. Did you remember a concluding sentence?
c. Please explain more about your holiday. Where did you stay? What did you do during the day?
d. I'm not sure what this part means.
e. I think this sentence should come before the next one.
f. I think these two sentences are really saying the same thing.
g. Your paragraph is about your brother, but this sentence is about your sister. Are you sure it's relevant?
h. I like your topic sentence because it has a strong main idea. Your example is funny. I wish I could meet your brother!

12
Answers will vary.

13
Paragraphs will vary.

14
False statements can be corrected in more than one way. Possible answers:
a. T
b. T
c. F; A detail is a specific description. An example is sometimes a short personal story.
d. F; The concluding sentence uses different words from the topic sentence.
e. F; The concluding sentence should not finish the paragraph with a new idea.
f. F; A peer editor should not mark any spelling or grammatical mistakes.
g. T
h. F; Peer editing helps the writer and the reader.
i. F; If a peer editor can't understand something that you wrote, then you know there may be a problem with his or her reading or your writing.
j. T

4 Descriptive and Process Paragraphs

Descriptive paragraphs

1
Answers will vary.

2
popular, beautiful, white, amazed, tree-lined, fast-moving, loud, roaring, cool, unforgettable

Describing the place around you

3
down the street from, on, in, on either side of, with, into, in, around, at, in, near, at, on, at, from, with, in

Describing a character

4
Answers will vary.

5
Answers will vary. Possible answers:

Personality	*Physical Characteristics*
shy	brown-, black-, blue-, green-eyed
quiet	muscular
talkative	petite
friendly	stocky

6
(not) big, tiny, thin, strong, happy, patient, good (advice), (I didn't need to be) afraid, (she never got) annoyed, interesting (stories), best (friend)

7
Answers will vary.

8
Answers will vary.

Process paragraphs

9

a. topic sentence: *Brown rice and vegetables is a simple and delicious meal to make.*
concluding sentence: *Now you are ready to enjoy your delicious brown rice and vegetables!*

b. 1. Cook the rice.
2. Cut the vegetables into one-inch pieces.
3. Heat the oil, chilli sauce, and garlic.
4. Add the vegetables and fry them.
5. Stir in the cooked rice.
6. Add salt and pepper.
7. Put the rice and vegetables into a bowl and serve with tomatoes and spring onions on top.

c. Transition words and phrases connect the sentences together.
First; Then; Next; After that; Now; After; Finally; Now

Transitions

10
Answers will vary. Possible answers:
now; when; at first; to begin / start with; first of all; afterwards; later; lastly

11
Answers will vary. Possible answers:
a. First / First of all
b. before
c. After
d. Next
e. While / When
f. next
g. Finally

Ordering sentences

12

a. 2	b. 4	c. 6	d. 5
e. 3	f. 7	g. 1	

13
Answers will vary.

Review

14
Paragraphs will vary. One possible answer:

I live next to a beautiful park. The park is quite large and has a lot of nice, green trees and grass. There is a small lake in the park where you can see people enjoying many different activities, such as swimming, fishing, boating, and other outdoor sports. In addition, there are many comfortable places to sit and relax. If you feel like walking or jogging, there are a lot of well-planned paths that you can take, and everywhere you go you can see beautiful flowers in all sorts of colours. I really enjoy spending time in this park.

5 Opinion Paragraphs

An opinion paragraph

1

a. The first sentence expresses the main idea.
b. The writer is trying to convince other people in his town to ride bicycles. He wrote the letter to show them why they should ride bicycles.
c. Sentences and phrases that show an opinion are: *More people should ride bicycles into town; Car traffic in town is terrible; parking places are hard to find; pollution from cars is a real problem; Citizens ... ought to try this non-polluting form of transport. Cycling is good exercise; The city must not allow this problem to get worse; people should ride bicycles to work and school.*
d. The writer included a fact (seventy-three percent of all workers drove their own car to work) to support his opinion.

2

Answers may vary.

a. O or B	e. F
b. O	f. O or B
c. F	g. B
d. B	h. O or B

3

Use opinions: editorials in newspapers and magazines, personal essays, restaurant reviews, etc.
Use facts: business reports, summaries or minutes of meetings, encyclopaedia entries, etc.

4

a. O	b. O	c. F	d. F
e. O	f. F	g. O	h. O

5

Answers will vary.

6

Answers will vary.

Modal auxiliaries

7

should; ought to; must not; should

8

a. should	b. can't	c. must
d. could	e. should	f. ought to

Expressing opinions: class survey

9

Answers will vary.

10

Answers will vary.

11

Answers will vary.

Connectors of cause and effect

12

Because petrol is becoming scarce and expensive, we should develop electric cars.
We should develop electric cars, since petrol is becoming scarce and expensive.
The transitions come before the causes.

Petrol is becoming scarce and expensive, so we should develop electric cars.
Petrol is becoming scarce and expensive. Therefore, we should develop electric cars.
The transitions come before the results.

13

a. , so
b. because *or* since
c. Because *or* Since
d. , so
e. , because *or* , since
f. Therefore,

14

a. The city doesn't have enough money, so we ought to increase council tax.
b. I'm going to leave my part-time job because I don't have enough time for my homework.
Because I don't have enough time for my homework, I'm going to leave my part-time job.
c. Some plants and trees have been dying since this summer has been very dry.
Since this summer has been very dry, some plants and trees have been dying.
d. Many students are graduating with nursing degrees. Therefore, it might be hard for nurses to find jobs in the future.
e. My friends all recommend that restaurant, so I will try it this weekend.

15
Answers will vary.

Writing an opinion paragraph

16
Paragraphs will vary.

Review

17

a. 8	b. 5	c. 11	d. 2	e. 9
f. 13	g. 4	h. 7	i. 6	j. 10
k. 1	l. 12	m. 3		

18
Paragraphs will vary; one possibility is given below.
Mobile phones should not be allowed in cinemas. For instance, last night, I went to see a film with my friend. It was a thriller. At the most exciting moment, the actors didn't speak, and only quiet music was playing. It was very exciting, so my friend and I leaned forward listening carefully. Suddenly, we heard a loud sound—a silly tune. The man behind us had a mobile phone, and he was receiving a call. In addition, he decided to answer it, so he spoke out loud to his friend. Because it was very distracting, my friend and I felt annoyed. Therefore, we feel that people should turn off their cell phones when they watch a film, or not bring them at all!

6 Comparison / Contrast Paragraphs

Choosing a topic

1
Answers will vary.

Comparing and contrasting

2
a. living with a host family and living in a flat in a hall of residence on the campus
b. Contrasting. The topic sentence in paragraph two says *but I want to live in a shared flat in a hall of residence on the campus*, which signals that contrasting ideas will be given. Also, transitions and transition phrases such as *on the other hand* and *However* show contrast.

Comparative and contrastive structures

3
a. similar to
b. Likewise, / Similarly,
c. Both ... and
d. as ... as

4
a. but / while / though
b. different from
c. On the other hand, / However,
d. more ... than

Similarities and differences

5
Possible sentences showing similarities:
Both cars have a clear 'For sale' sign.
Another similarity between the two cars is that they are both made in Germany.
Car 1 is the same colour as car 2.
A dog is sitting in the passenger seat of car 1. Likewise, car 2 has a dog sitting in the passenger seat.

Possible sentences describing differences:
Car 1 has four doors, while car 2 has only two.
Car 2 is £100,000, but car 1 is only £1,000.
Car 2 is smaller than car 1.
The top speed of car 1 is 50 mph. On the other hand, car 2's top speed is 150 mph.

Comparison / contrast organization

6
a. Paragraph 1 mostly contrasts, and Paragraph 2 mostly compares.
b. Outline for Paragraph 1:

Topic A—reading a book
1. Use imagination; descriptions of people, places, things let you see the pictures in your mind.
2. Conversations with descriptions of how people look or feel let you create the characters in your mind.

Topic B—seeing a film
1. Imagination not needed; pictures on screen give all necessary details.
2. Conversations are spoken aloud, so just watch and listen; feelings of people come from their faces, bodies, voices.

Outline for Paragraph 2:

First point of comparison—difficult childhood
A1: Monroe—many years in orphanage
B1: Diana—mother left family

Second point of comparison—later lives—married famous men
A1: Diana—married Prince Charles; separated
B1: Monroe—married famous baseball player, famous writer; separated
Third point of comparison—popular
A1: Diana—friendly, called 'The people's princess'
B1: Monroe—sexy but well-liked, seemed innocent
Fourth point of comparison —had emotional problems
A1: Monroe—serious depression, went to hospital for help
B1: Diana—eating problem, had depression
Fifth point of comparison—deaths
A1: Monroe—died in 1962 at age 36
B1: Diana—died in 1997 at age 36

7

The second paragraph in exercise 2 on page 41 uses point-by-point organisation.
first point—living arrangements and freedom
second point—food

8

Similarities
- Played outdoors.
- Played with at least two people.
- Both men and women play.
- A ball is hit.
- Accuracy is important.

Differences
- Tennis can also be played indoors.
- Tennis is played on a court with a net.
- Golf is played on a large area.
- Tennis uses a racket to hit a ball.
- Golf uses clubs to hit a ball.
- Tennis is fairly cheap to play.
- Golf is expensive to play in some countries.
- Speed is an important skill for tennis.

9

Paragraphs will vary.

Advantages and disadvantages

10

The paragraph discusses the advantages of studying abroad and in your own country.
Supporting points:
living in another country:
- exciting, new, and different
- challenging; therefore, develops courage and self-confidence
- great way to learn another language
- good way to learn about another culture

staying in own country:
- cheaper; therefore, can save money
- everything is familiar; no need to study in another language; culture and expectations of classes are clear
- close to family and friends

11

Paragraphs will vary.

12

Answers will vary.

13

a. D b. A c. D d. A e. A
f. D g. D h. A i. A j. D

14

Paragraphs will vary.

7 Problem / Solution Paragraphs

Problems and solutions

1

- The main idea of the first paragraph is that deforestation is a problem.
- The topic sentence is the first one, *Deforestation is a serious problem because forests and trees aren't just pretty to look at, they do an important job of making the earth's environment suitable for life.*

2

a. The first paragraph is developed by details. The supporting ideas are that trees clean the air, store water, preserve soil, and provide homes for animals; that trees supply food, fuel, wood products, and paper products; that deforestation may change the climate, cause floods, and cause the death of animals.

b. The supporting ideas show the importance of trees.
c. The main idea of the second paragraph is that individuals can prevent deforestation by using less paper. The topic sentence is the fourth one, *Here's one simple suggestion that everyone can try: use less paper.*
d. The writer offers one solution to deforestation: *Use less paper.* The writer offers three ways to do this: *reduce, reuse, and recycle.*
e. Both paragraphs have concluding sentences (the last sentence of each paragraph).

Writing about problems

3

Answers will vary.

4

if deforestation continues, the world's climate may change ...; ... if a lot of people make small changes in their lifestyle, the effect can be great; If you use less paper, fewer trees will be cut for paper making; If you follow the three Rs—reduce, reuse, and recycle—you can help save the world's forests.

5

a. use; could get
b. will do; don't get
c. want; exercise; don't eat
d. fly; will be
e. can be; think
f. will go; find

6

Answers will vary.

7

Answers will vary.

8

Paragraphs will vary.

Linking problems with solutions

9

One solution to the problem of deforestation is to ...
One answer is to ...
A second answer is to ...
A final answer is to ...

10

Answers will vary.

Writing solutions

11

Answers will vary. Possible answers are:

- borrow money from my friends: weak
- sell some of my things: OK
- ask my parents for money: OK
- go busking with my guitar: weak
- get a part-time job: strong
- drop out of university and get a full-time job: weak
- buy lottery tickets: weak
- ride my bike to university instead of using public transport: strong
- ask my lecturers for money: weak
- buy fewer CDs and new clothes: strong

12

Paragraphs will vary.

13

Answers will vary.

Review

14

Additional problems and solutions will vary.

problems	solutions
noisy flatmate	make cleaning rota
flatmate is messy	set aside quiet time for studying
argue about how to decorate flat	each person decorates half of the flat
fighting causes stress	talk each week about concerns

15

Paragraphs will vary.

8 The Structure of an Essay

The structure of an essay

1

Introduction: first paragraph
Main body paragraphs: second and third paragraphs
Conclusion: fourth paragraph

Thesis statements

2

The thesis statement is the last one in the first paragraph: *African Americans, too, have both contributed new words to English and changed the meanings of some existing words.*

3

a. Thesis statement: *The UK can be divided into different regions that each has its own characteristic foods influenced by cultures of the people who live there.*
Topic: British food
Main idea: Each region has its own characteristic foods influenced by the cultures of the people who live there.

b. Thesis statement: *As a result of human population growth, deforestation and hunting, the number of koalas has declined.*
Topic: koalas
Main idea: number declining due to human population growth, deforestation and hunting

c. Thesis statement: *No two Taoist gardens are exactly alike, but all Taoist gardens include four essential elements: water, mountains, buildings, and bridges.*
Topic: Taoist gardens
Main idea: all Taoist gardens include the elements water, mountains, buildings, and bridges

4

a. F	b. N	c. F	d. ✓	e. N
f. F	g. ✓	h. N	i. F	j. ✓

Writing thesis statements

5

a. Main body paragraphs: one paragraph per region, describing what the food and culture in each region is like and how it is different from the others

b. Main body paragraphs: three paragraphs that each discuss one of the three causes for koala bears' decline—human population growth, deforestation, and hunting

c. Main body paragraphs: four paragraphs that each discuss one of the four elements—water, mountains, buildings, and bridges

6

Answers will vary.

7

Answers will vary.

8

Answers will vary.

Review

9

1. main
2. paragraph
3. idea
4. essay
5. supporting
6. main body
7. concluding
8. conclusion

9 Outlining an Essay

Looking at an outline

1

a. *Nuclear power is not a good energy source for the world.*

b. It will have three paragraphs in the main body.

c. The third paragraph will have two supporting points: *Nuclear fuels are dangerous* and *Nuclear waste products are dangerous.*

d. There will be eight details in the fourth paragraph: *Three Mile Island, USA (1979); Tarapur, India (1992); Darlington, Canada (1992); Chernobyl, USSR (1986); Kola, Russia (1991); Tokaimura, Japan (1999); Earthquake: Kozloduy, Bulgaria (1977); Tornado: Moruroa, the Pacific (1981).*

Writing an outline

2

I. Thesis statement: *African Americans, too, have both contributed new words to English and changed the meanings of some existing words.*

II. Words introduced by *African Americans (who came as slaves)*
  A. *OK*
    1. From an African language
    2. Now used all over the world to mean *all right*
  B. *Jazz*
    1. Came from African American musicians in New Orleans
    2. Exact origin unknown

III. Words whose meanings changed over time
  A. *Cool*
    1. Original meaning
    2. New meanings
  B. *Square*
    1. Original meaning
    2. New meaning

IV. *Conclusion:* Existing ethnic groups in the

United States as well as new immigrants will certainly continue to bring new words to English and give fresh meanings to existing words.

3

a. S b. M c. S d. S e. M f. S g. S
h. S i. S j. T k. S l. C m. M

4

I. Doing yoga regularly can be good for your mind, your body, and your emotions.
II. Mental benefits
  A. Develops clear thinking
  B. Improves concentration
III. Physical benefits
  A. Makes you strong and flexible
  B. Improves blood circulation
  C. Improves digestion
IV. Emotional benefits
  A. Develops self-confidence
  B. Reduces fear, anger, and worry
  C. Helps you feel calm and peaceful
V. Therefore, to build mental, physical, and emotional health, consider doing yoga.

Evaluating an outline

5

I. • OK.
II. • Points B and C should be swapped (dates in the wrong order).
  • Point E should be deleted (not relevant).
III.
  • III and IV should be swapped.
  • Point A might include a second category of people who come to San Francisco to get rich.
  • Point B should be deleted (not relevant).
  • Point C3 should be deleted (not relevant).
  • Point D could be more specific.
  • Point F should be deleted (not a separate subpoint; it might be mentioned in a topic sentence, however).
  • Point G could be more specific.
IV. • Point B should discuss expenses for food and clothing (to be parallel with the section on San Francisco today).
V. • OK.

6

Answers will vary.

7

Answers will vary.

Review

8

Answers will vary. Sample answer:

I. Mary enjoys both indoor and outdoor hobbies.
II. Indoor hobbies
  A. Reading
    1. Novels
    2. Poetry
  B. Sewing
  C. Listening to music
    1. Pop
    2. Jazz
III. Outdoor hobbies
  A. Walking
    1. Mountain climbing
    2. Around town
  B. Bird watching
  C. Canoeing
IV. Both Mary's indoor and outdoor hobbies are activities that she enjoys doing by herself.

9

Answers will vary.

10

Answers will vary.

10 Introductions and Conclusions

The introduction

1

Line 1: English has been influenced by other countries and groups.
Line 2: Some words are borrowed from other languages.
Lines 3 and 4: African Americans have contributed and changed words.

2

Answers may vary.

a. ✗—Too short. The writer could add one or two more sentences with information about changes in families. Also, there is no interesting information to draw the reader in. Some statistics or examples could be added at the beginning.
b. ✓
c. ✗—The introduction doesn't have a thesis statement. A possible thesis statement: *Stargazing is a valuable way to learn about our world as well as outer space.* If a different thesis statement is chosen, some of the details in the introduction may be too specific or not relevant.
d. ✗—Too long, with some information that is not relevant. The writer should delete *These cities are popular tourist destinations with many interesting sights* and *Jazz originated in the American South in the early twentieth century.*
e. ✗—Too short; also, the sentences are not related closely enough. One of the ideas needs to be chosen and developed into an introductory paragraph.

Types of information

3

a. personal experience
b. facts
c. facts, an interesting quotation

4

Answers will vary.

The conclusion

5

a. The conclusion restates the thesis and makes a final comment about the essay's main idea.
b. The first sentence, 'English owes some of its interesting and colourful vocabulary to African Americans' restates the thesis statement.

6

a. 3 b. 1 c. 5 d. 2 e. 6 f. 4

7

Paragraph *b* is the best concluding paragraph. Paragraph *a* discusses health problems and paragraph *c* discusses how immigrants bring customs from their native countries to Britain. Only *b* summarises the information about how British food has been influenced by other cultures.

8

Answers will vary.

Review

9

1. interest
2. facts
3. story
4. quotation
5. topic
6. information
7. thesis
8. summarises
9. restates
10. comment
11. action

10

Answers will vary.

11 Unity and Coherence

Unity in writing

1

a. Thesis statement: *The philosophy of Chinese medicine is not the same as the philosophy of modern medicine, but it is useful for curing many health problems.*
b. Topic sentences:
First main body paragraph: *Modern medicine focuses on illness.*
Second main body paragraph: *Instead of focusing on a patient's health problems, Chinese medicine tries to make the patient's whole body well again.*
c. Supporting ideas:
First main body paragraph:
- In modern medicine, a patient with a cough gets medicine to stop the cough.
- Different medicine given for fever.
- Same medicine given to all people.

- Philosophy of modern medicine—stop problems quickly.

Second main body paragraph:
- Chinese medicine—two types of energy in people.
- One type is yin (passive).
- Second type is yang (active).
- Healthy when there is equal balance of energy.
- Imbalance means person is unhealthy.
- Don't stop illness by giving medicine.
- Herbs given to restore balance, so illness stops naturally.

d. The essay is unified.

Editing an essay for unity

2

The text that should be removed is the following: All the sentences beginning from *Another Frenchman, Louis Braille* ... to ... *a training school for teachers of the deaf.* These sentences don't relate to the topic of the essay, which is *sign language.*

Coherence in writing

3

The essay in exercise 1 uses comparison / contrast organisation. The topic of modern medicine is contrasted with Chinese medicine. It has block style organisation.

The essay in exercise 2 has chronological organisation. The main body paragraphs are organised by different periods in history.

Cohesive devices

4

Answers will vary. Possible answers:
1. Instead
2. Specifically / In particular
3. for example / for instance
4. Instead / Rather
5. As a result / Therefore / Thus

5

a. the city / Barcelona
b. Barcelona
c. the Barrio Góticos / Barri Gòtics
d. Barcelona's
e. Catalan speakers in and around Barcelona
f. in Barcelona
g. all of the previous supporting points in the paragraph

6

- transition use—first, another, and
- pronoun reference—these signs (the signs used by a group of deaf people in Paris); he (L'Epée, Thomas Gallaudet); this time (in 1815, travelling in Europe); it (American Sign Language)
- repetition of key words—sign language / signs, deaf, developed / development

7

Answers will vary.
Ho Chi Minh City, *located on the Mekong River* in Vietnam, is a fascinating destination for travellers to Southeast Asia. It was once an important trading centre for the French in Southeast Asia, *and* the influence of French culture can still be felt. *For example*, many people, especially the older generations, learned French in school and still can speak it very well. *In addition*, some cafés serve French-style bread and pastries in Ho Chi Minh City, *and* expensive hotels and restaurants serve French food. *Another sign of French influence* is that many of the buildings in the city are built in French style. There are *also* many museums and monuments documenting the country's long—and often bloody—history. The Vietnamese and the French *also* fought, *but* the French eventually left the country. If you're looking for a unique city to visit in Southeast Asia, Ho Chi Minh City is an attractive choice.

8

Answers will vary.

9

Answers will vary.

10

Answers will vary.

Review

11

a. 1. before
   Meaning: Don't think about future rewards (such as money) until they actually appear.
b. 2. When
   Meaning: If you are facing a bad or difficult situation, try to make something good from it.
c. 3. when
   Meaning: Time passes very quickly when you are enjoying yourself.
d. 2. but

Meaning: You can suggest an idea or give someone advice, but you cannot make the person listen to or follow the advice.

e. 2. and, and
Meaning: People prefer to be around someone who is in a good mood.

f. 3. until
Meaning: You don't know how important something is to you until you lose it.

12
Answers will vary.

12 Essays for Examinations

Timed essays

1
Answers will vary. Possible answers:

a. Students' own answers
b. Students' own answers
c. For university entrance examinations; for tests in English classes; for tests in subject-matter classes taught in English
d. Pressure is increased; less time is spent on preparing and checking your work; no peer feedback; only one draft is written
e. Students' own answers

Instructions for timed essays

2
Answers will vary. Possible answers:

a. <u>Compare and contrast</u> state and private secondary school education in your country.
b. Think of a story you have read which has also been made into a film. <u>Describe the differences</u> between the two versions.
c. <u>Show how</u> the rise in popularity of communication by mobile phone has <u>changed</u> the ways in which young people communicate.
d. <u>Discuss three results</u> of the Norman conquest of Britain in 1066. Which do you feel was the <u>most important</u>?
e. <u>Which</u> environmental problem is the <u>most significant</u> in your community? <u>Explain</u> how your community can <u>solve</u> this problem.

Answering directly

3
Answers will vary. Possible answer:
<u>Which effect</u> of the California gold rush do you think had the <u>biggest impact</u> on the character of San Francisco today?

4

a. ✗ There are too many general sentences (*San Francisco is a fascinating city ...; Each year, thousands of tourists ... Many important events ...*). This would be OK in an essay written as coursework, but takes too much time in a test situation and is not relevant information. In addition, the writer does not say which effect of the gold rush was the most important.
b. ✓ It answers the question clearly and directly.
c. ✗ The first sentence is too general. The writer doesn't clearly state which effect of the gold rush was the most important; the use of *for example* makes it sound like the writer will also discuss other effects. *It was a very exciting time* is not necessary.
d. ✗ The writer lists many effects of the gold rush, but does not choose the most important one.
e. ✓ It answers the question clearly and directly.

Managing your time

5
Answers will vary.

6
Answers will vary.

Checking your work

7
Answers will vary.

Review

8
Answers will vary.

Photocopiable Materials

Writing survey

1. Answer the questions.

a. What types of writing do you do in your native language at least once a month? Add to the list.

❒ letters	❒ essays
❒ lists	❒ ....
❒ e-mail	❒ ....
❒ diary	❒ ....

b. What type of writing is the most enjoyable? What type is the least enjoyable? Why?

c. How often do you write in English? What do you write in English?

d. Will you write in English in the future? What kinds of things will you write?

e. When you write:

	yes	no
Do you write with pencil and paper?	❒	❒
Do you use a computer?	❒	❒
Do you use a dictionary?	❒	❒
Do you make notes before you write?	❒	❒
Do you write your text in your native language first?	❒	❒
Do you write your text more than once?	❒	❒

f. How easy are these things when you write in English? Circle the most appropriate number. (1 = very easy, 2 = quite easy, 3 = quite challenging, 4 = very challenging)

grammar	1	2	3	4
expressing myself	1	2	3	4
vocabulary / finding the right word	1	2	3	4
getting ideas	1	2	3	4
writing something interesting	1	2	3	4
writing something beautiful	1	2	3	4
writing something original	1	2	3	4
writing something intellectual	1	2	3	4

g. What do you hope to learn from this class?

2. Share your answers with a partner or small group.

Peer feedback—paragraph

Writer's name:
Reader's name:

Assignment:

1. What is the topic of the paragraph? What is the main idea?

2. Does the paragraph have a topic sentence? If so, write it here.

3. Does each sentence support the topic sentence? If not, which sentence or sentences do not belong?

4. Does the paragraph have a concluding sentence? If so, does it restate the topic sentence or sum up the information?

5. Are there any places where the writer could add more details? Do you have any questions for the writer?

6. What are some good things about this paragraph?

Peer feedback—essay

Writer's name:
Reader's name:

Assignment:

1. What is the topic of the essay? What is the main idea?

2. Read the introduction. Is it interesting? Does it give some background information? Does it include a thesis statement? If so, write it here:

3. Does each paragraph in the main body support the thesis statement? Write the topic sentence of each paragraph in the main body here:

4. Are there any places where the writer could add more details? Do you have any questions for the writer?

5. Is there a conclusion to the essay? Does it restate the thesis or sum up the information or flow logically from the ideas in the essay? Does it contain any new points?

6. What are some good things about this essay?

Paragraph evaluation form

Writer:

Assignment: Final mark:

	Comments	Mark
Topic sentence / main idea		
Paragraph unity		
Paragraph coherence		
Language use		
Strengths of the paragraph		
Weaknesses of the paragraph		

Essay evaluation form

Writer:

Assignment: Final mark:

	Comments	Mark
Introduction / thesis statement		
Main body paragraphs		
Essay unity and coherence		
Conclusion		
Language use		
Strengths of the essay		
Weaknesses of the essay		

PHOTOCOPIABLE

Error log chart

Assignment										
Type of error										
sp										
wf										
wc										
wo										
sing										
pl										
art										
inf										
?										
pron										
s / v										
v-tense										
v-form										
v-pass										
cs										
ro										
frag										
co										
infin / ger										
x										
prep										
punct										
c										
¶										
^										

Error code

The symbols from the error log chart are explained below with an example sentence given for each type of error. The correction is given in brackets.

sp = spelling	The boy was afeared of the dog. (afraid)
wf = word form	They were education in many different countries. (educated)
wc = word choice	We bought the rug after describing the price. (discussing)
wo = word order	Amanda is reading always on her bed. (is always reading)
sing = singular noun	John works as an investment brokers. (broker)
pl = plural noun	There are many advantage of living abroad. (advantages)
art = article	A enthusiastic employee is an asset for a company. (An)
inf = too informal	The committee is not gonna change the plans of the project. (going to)
? = meaning unclear	The government plans to create every child goes to school. (plans to create a fund allowing every child to go to school)
pron = pronoun	The company's profits continue to be good, so it will expand your product line. (its)
s / v = subject / verb agreement	Several people from my country attends the class. (attend)
v-tense = verb tense	Last year, we go to visit relatives in a neighbouring city. (went)
v-form = verb form	I will be go to the dentist next week. (will go)
v-pass = passive verb	The workers forced to work for twelve hours by management. (were forced)
cs = comma splice	The shop ended its sale, it marked up the remaining goods. (... sale, and it ...)
ro = run-on sentence	If the temperature drops, the lake will freeze last year it froze for several months. (... freeze. Last year ...)
frag = fragment	Because the cinema was old and no longer in use. (Because ... in use, it was closed and the property was sold.)
co = connecting word	*Examples:* While we finished dinner, we went to meet the new neighbours. (After) The laboratory lacks modern equipment, or it is still used for many experiments. (but)
inf / ger = infinitive / gerund	The law attempts ending smoking in all public buildings. (to end)
line through word = delete	Several countries have signed ~~to~~ the peace treaty. (... have signed the peace treaty.)
prep = preposition	Donations were given into the charity. (to)
punct = punctuation	The summer is long hot and humid. (... long, hot, and ...)
c = capitalisation	Number 10 Downing Street is the place of residence for the prime minister of the UK. (Number 10 Downing Street)
¶ = start a new paragraph	
^ = add a word	Completion^the project is expected in six to eight months. (Completion of the project ...) (prep)

PHOTOCOPIABLE

Error log exercises

1. Correct the errors in the following sentences.

a. Casinos attracting elderly people by offering them free gifts.
(v-form)

b. Football and American football are both very exciting game for spectators.
(pl)

c. Watching too much television can have ^ negative effect on children.
(art)

d. She concerns about the amount of money she spends with credit cards.
(v-pass)

e. Although the population is increasing in larger cities.
(frag)

f. The first step in applying to a university is to completion an application form.
(wf)

g. In the past ten years, most of the country's revenue will be spent on construction of the new transport system.
(v-tense)

h. Lecturers are expekted to mark students' work fairly.
(sp)

2. Find six errors in the following paragraph and correct them:
inf / ger, v-form, wc, pl, wf, and ^.

Regularly exercise helps people's physical and mental health. In particular, active exercises like cycling, playing basketball, to jog, playing tennis, or walking can all be especially helpful for people's health. When people do these types of exercise three to five time per week, they can received many benefits such as reducing their weight, decreasing their blood pressure and heart rate, and getting stronger muscles. Moreover, exercise helps people feel better mentally because it can help reduce feelings of sadness, anger, or worry. There are certain chemicals in the brain that increase during people exercise, and this often makes them feel happier. With regular exercise, people can take care themselves and enjoy a better life.

Error log exercises answer key

Answers

1 a. attract
b. games
c. a
d. is concerned
e. Answers will vary. Answers should be full sentences
f. complete
g. was spent
h. expected

2 inf / ger: line 2, *to jog* ➔ *jogging*
v-form: line 3, *received* ➔ *receive*
wc: line 6, *during* ➔ *when*
pl: line 3, *time* ➔ *times*
wf: line 1, *Regularly* ➔ *Regular*
^ line 7, *care themselves* ➔ *care of themselves*

Macmillan Education
4 Crinan Street
London N1 9XW
A division of Macmillan Publishers Limited
Companies and representatives throughout the world

ISBN 978-1-4050-8606-6

First published 2003
This edition 2005

Designed by Glynis Edwards
Project managed by Lewis Lansford
Illustrated by Jackson Graham, Sophie Grillet, Stuart Perry
Cover design by Andrew Oliver
Cover photo by Stock Connection Distribution/Alamy

Authors' acknowledgements
Dorothy E. Zemach thanks students in the Academic English for International Students writing courses at the University of Oregon, who tried out many of the exercises in the book and provided valuable comments and suggestions. Special thanks to Lewis Lansford and David Williamson. Before I started writing, I used to wonder why authors thanked editors. But now I know!

Lisa A. Rumisek thanks Lisa von Reichbauer, instructor in the English Language Institute at Central Michigan University and the students in the Intensive English program who kindly helped pilot many of the exercises in the book and provided helpful comments and suggestions. Special thanks to Lewis Lansford and David Williamson.
The publishers would like to thank the following for their assistance in the development of this course (in alphabetical order):
Stuart Bowie, Kevin Cleary, Chris Cottam, Clyde Fowle, Takashi Hata, Jeong Sook Lee, Pearl Lin, Steve Maginn, David Parker, Thawatchai Pattarawongvisut, Cristina Roberts, Gordon Robson, Satoshi Saito, Maria-Luiza Santos, Sandra Wu, Jinsoo Yoon

The authors and publishers would like to thank the following for permission to reproduce the following photographic material: Alamy pp26 ©Glen Allison, 84 ©Johan Furusjo; Corbis pp28 ©Jed and Kaoru Share, 30 ©Stuart Westmorland, 33 ©Anne W. Krausel, 38 ©Paul Barton, 58 ©r-f Corbis, 75(tm) ©Layne Kennedy; Edifice p25(r) ©I Dunnel; Empics p15; Getty Images: p76 ©Richard L'Anson/Lonely Planet Images: Stone pp25(l), 51, 60, 66, 75(tl, bm), 78/9: Taxi pp17, 65, 92: The Imagebank pp75(r); Sally & Richard Greenhill Photographers p14; LondonStills ©www.londonstills.com p32; Photolibrary.com p11; Rex Features p37; Topham Picturepoint p68; Travel Ink p86 ©Travel Ink/Colin Marshall.

Printed and bound in Thailand

2019 2018 2017 2016
19 18 17 16 15 14 13